The Diary of an Old Soul

by

George MacDonald

&

The White Page Poems

by

Betty K. Aberlin

Zossima Press

ISBN 0-972322-140

10 - 9 - 8 - 7 - 6 - 5 - 4 - 3 - 2

Psalm 126

A Song of Ascents.

When the Lord restored the fortunes of Zion,
we were like those who dream.
Then our mouth was filled with laughter,
and our tongue with shouts of joy;
then it was said among the nations,
"The Lord has done great things for them."
The Lord has done great things for us,
and we rejoiced.
Restore our fortunes, O Lord,
like the watercourses in the Negeb.
May those who sow in tears
reap with shouts of joy.
Those who go out weeping,
bearing the seed for sowing,
shall come home with shouts of joy,
carrying their sheaves.

The New Year

Be welcome, year! With corn and sickle come;
Make poor the body, but make rich the heart:
What man that bears his sheaves, gold-nodding, home
Will heed the paint rubbed from his groaning cart!

Nor leave behind thy fears and holy shames,
Thy sorrows on the horizon hanging low –
Gray gathered fuel for the sunset-flames
When joyous in death's harvest-home we go.

George MacDonald
from A Threefold Cord (1883)

Introduction

George MacDonald (1824-1905) was a Scottish writer of numerous novels, wonder-stories, fantasy, literary criticism, sermons, and poetry. Sometimes referred to as the father of Christian fantasy, MacDonald influenced such prominent twentieth century writers as G.K. Chesterton, J.R.R. Tolkien, C.S. Lewis and Madeline L'Engle.

MacDonald privately published 366 seven-line poems in 1880 as *A Book of Strife in the Form of the Diary of an Old Soul*. No stranger to hardship, MacDonald suffered from emphysema, eczema, bouts of depression, and poverty throughout his long life. Several times poor health placed him at the point of death. His mother died when he was 10 and his two closest brothers died as young men. He outlived 4 of his 11 children, 2 of whom died in 1878 and 1879, the period just before the publication of these daily poems. Readers of MacDonald's books, filled as they are with hope and optimism, might be surprised to learn of the many tests of faith God permitted during his life.

MacDonald's poetry and poetic theories are contained in nearly everything he wrote. His first book *Within and Without* (1855), a dramatic poem, attracted the attention of Lady Byron, widow of the poet. He translated the *Spiritual Songs* of Novalis in 1851 and was an early admirer of Robert Browning. He became personally acquainted with Tennyson who, in turn, was an admirer of MacDonald's theological mentor F.D. Maurice. Tennyson dedicated his poem *Maud* to Maurice in 1855. Maurice and MacDonald were both deeply indebted to S.T. Coleridge and MacDonald was so fascinated with *The Rime of the Ancient Mariner*, he made it the subject of a chapter in the novel *There and Back*.

Over the course of MacDonald's career four volumes of his collected poems were published plus a book about the religious poetry of England called *England's Antiphon* (1867) and a critical study, *The Tragedy of Hamlet* (1885). MacDonald was also a frequent and popular lecturer and his subject matter was almost invariably about poets and poetry. Dante, Shakespeare, Robert Burns, Tennyson, and Wordsworth were among his favorite topics, often drawing thousands of listeners in auditoriums across England, Ireland, Scotland, and during his 1872-3 lecture tour, in America.

Despite the centrality of poetry in MacDonald's career, little study has been devoted to this aspect of his writing. Perhaps the earliest compiler of MacDonald's poetry was the American scholar Vida Dutton Scudder, a renowned professor of Medieval and Renaissance literature as well as an expert on Victorian poetry. Her essay introducing MacDonald's poetry in 1887 does not mention *The Diary of an Old Soul*. However, her eloquent description of MacDonald's poetry applies equally to the poems contained in this book:

> In the treatment of the spiritual life these poems possess a quality even more noticeable and unique than their honesty of vision; it is their subtle power with which they delineate certain less obvious phases of nature and experience. Of the morbid analysis into which this subtlety sometimes leads – or sometimes misleads – the poems show no trace. From this he is saved by his wholesomeness of vision on the one hand, and on the other by the fact that with him religious emotion always finds its basis in clear intellectual perception. [The poems] do not merely reflect and enhance in melodious numbers a pleasing sentiment, but afford real guidance and helpfulness in some of those unrecognized perplexities that press upon the bewildered soul in its efforts to commune with the unseen. These perplexities, underlying as they do our keenest spiritual sorrow and joy, are seldom touched by religious verse except in their most obvious aspects; they are rendered by Mr. MacDonald with sympathetic and accurate penetration; and therefore it is that they possess an enduring value. He is one of those authors . . . who make less solitary the inmost recesses of the spiritual life.

Over the years *Diary* gained admirers from comparatively few readers, obscured as it has been by MacDonald's more famous and popular works. But the laudatory reviews are significant. John Ruskin called it "one of the three great sacred poems of the nineteenth century." C.S. Lewis wrote to Owen Barfield, saying the poem was "magnificent."

According to Walter Hooper, C.S. Lewis owned a "new edition" of the poems published in 1885. The poems were printed again in a collection entitled *Rampoli*, MacDonald's last published book in 1897. Later editions were printed in 1905 (reprinted 1909, 1914) and by Augsburg Publishing in 1975. Later editions differ from the original in several ways. First, the title was abbreviated to *The Diary of an Old Soul*. Second, in the 1880 book the pages opposite the poems were intentionally left blank. MacDonald wrote a "Dedication" poem encouraging his readers to write their own thoughts on the empty "white page."

Another difference in recent editions of *Diary* is the exclusion of the epilogue poem MacDonald added in the 1897 *Rampoli* version. The first line of that poem (p.194) may refer to MacDonald's increasing silence due to diminished mental faculties. But it also suggests a chosen, holy silence of listening and waiting upon God. The last of his many psalm-like poems of struggle and resignation, MacDonald is waiting for death. He anticipates that after this life his sins *"shall be revealed"* and therefore places his hope in the efficacy of *"cleansing sorrow."*

The book you are reading now restores the dedication and epilogue poems. The blank "white pages" have been filled with corresponding poems by Betty Aberlin. The result fulfills MacDonald's original intention – that his readers interact deeply with these personal devotional poems. After reading the two poems in tandem, readers may find they respond more deeply than when reading one of the poems alone. Betty shares with MacDonald a refreshing honesty and closeness to nature that often illuminates the original poem, expands it with new insights, and provides the reader with additional points of reference for their own spiritual examination.

The Diary of an Old Soul is presented with *The White Page Poems* in the hope that you will:

"Grow with Old Soul in your own time and place."

Open your heart and mind, find a blank diary to write in and be prepared to *"Receive anew the invitation grace."*

Robert Trexler, publisher

The stars are threshed, and the souls
are threshed from their husks.

W. B. Yeats

And I must enter again the round
Zion of the water bead
And the synagogue of the ear of corn

Dylan Thomas

The Diary of an Old Soul

DEDICATION

Sweet friends, receive my offering. You will find
Against each worded page a white page set: –
This is the mirror of each friendly mind
Reflecting that. In this book we are met.
Make it, dear hearts, of worth to you indeed: –
Let your white page be ground, my print be seed,
Growing to golden ears, that faith and hope shall feed.

YOUR OLD SOUL

The White Page Poems

DEDICATION

Here are the golden ears of harvest ground,
Threshed out of grief, that what was lost be found: –
Dear unknown friends, you who now read and see,
Receive anew the invitation grace.
Grow with Old Soul in your own time and place: –
May it be sweet as is his love to me –
Daily communion in Eternity.

bka

JANUARY.

1.

LORD, what I once had done with youthful might,
Had I been from the first true to the truth,
Grant me, now old, to do – with better sight,
And humbler heart, if not the brain of youth;
So wilt thou, in thy gentleness and ruth,
Lead back thy old soul, by the path of pain,
Round to his best – young eyes and heart and brain.

2.

A dim aurora rises in my east,
Beyond the line of jagged questions hoar,
As if the head of our intombed High Priest
Began to glow behind the unopened door:
Sure the gold wings will soon rise from the gray ! –
They rise not. Up I rise, press on the more,
To meet the slow coming of the Master's day.

3.

Sometimes I wake, and, lo! I have forgot,
And drifted out upon an ebbing sea!
My soul that was at rest now resteth not,
For I am with myself and not with thee;
Truth seems a blind moon in a glaring morn,
Where nothing is but sick-heart vanity:
Oh, thou who knowest! save thy child forlorn.

JANUARY

1/1

LORD, may this incense ceaselessly arise.
Receive this prayer in which I join my soul
Now, spiraling beyond time, within, world
Without end. By silences, windfalls, sighs,
By pain or plenty, poverty, grief, coal
Or primrose, refine us. Our guide is wise.
North star of January, make us whole!

1/2

Weighed down by fear that masquerades as rage –
An enemy I must sit *shiva* for –
I let go now, and enter a new age
Of real uncertainty. In pastel dawn,
With silent questions deep inside the core.
I choose to rise, to lose all, to adore;
To marvel at the rabbit on the lawn.

1/3

Dead whales and oil slicks edge the seas this year,
As you in silence wait to meet your death.
This rainy morn' the thorns bloom plastic bags
Blown from the dump and waving in the drear.
So peace and stillness, precious as each breath,
Distill truth-seeking as the tide drags
Us out into the deep: Lord, save and hear!

4.

Death, like high faith, levelling, lifteth all.
When I awake, my daughter and my son,
Grown sister and brother, in my arms shall fall,
Tenfold my girl and boy. Sure every one
Of all the brood to the old wings will run.
Whole-hearted is my worship of the man
From whom my earthly history began.

5.

Thy fishes breathe but where thy waters roll;
Thy birds fly but within thy airy sea;
My soul breathes only in thy infinite soul;
I breathe, I think, I love, I live but thee.
Oh breathe, oh think, – O Love, live into me;
Unworthy is my life till all divine,
Till thou see in me only what is thine.

6.

Then shall I breathe in sweetest sharing, then
Think in harmonious consort with my kin;
Then shall I love well all my father's men,
Feel one with theirs the life my heart within.
Oh brothers! sisters holy! hearts divine!
Then I shall be all yours, and nothing mine –
To every human heart a mother-twin.

7.

I see a child before an empty house,
Knocking and knocking at the closed door;
He wakes dull echoes – but nor man nor mouse,
If he stood knocking there for evermore. –
A mother angel, see! folding each wing,
Soft-walking, crosses straight the empty floor,
And opens to the obstinate praying thing.

1/4

Ah, George, your faith is perfect, unlike mine.
I sense my kin beyond attend me now,
But as for august Death, he is a sign
Before which I can only (awestruck) bow.
I am too small to look into this *tao*.
What heaven is, I can't conceive or see;
Nor can I know what God has planned for me.

1/5

Today I was a shoveler in your snow;
The Holy Church of Snow, I shoveled, prayed;
I bend to dig and – *thank you!* – lift to throw.
In work and love my mind on you is stayed.
My heart and lungs and will are in your braid.
Yes, live in me, that I be rightly mended,
And incarnate the nature you intended.

1/6

The trees and rocks a-glitter now with ice
Brilliant with sunlight, prisms upon which
A small bird hops, waiting for me to fill
The feeders – ice tears slowly fall. Advice
And wisdom chip away my frozen niche
In winter rock. I surrender, hold still;
Melt me, please, good Lord – let me do thy will.

1/7

I see a girl, deep in a fairy-tale,
Longing and pining for an angel dad.
Beside this book-life, her own life is pale.
She mourns the loss of that she never had.
Years pass; a demon-lover takes her on,
She sees God!/is rejected, driven mad;
Lord's grace arrives when every *else* is gone.

8.

Were there but some deep, holy spell, whereby
Always I should remember thee – some mode
Of feeling the pure heat-throb momently
Of the spirit-fire still uttering this *I!* –
Lord, see thou to it, take thou remembrance' load:
Only when I bethink me can I cry;
Remember thou, and prick me with love's goad.

9.

If to myself – "God sometimes interferes" –
I said, my faith at once would be struck blind.
I see him all in all, the lifing mind,
Or nowhere in the vacant miles and years.
A love he is that watches and that hears,
Or but a mist fumed up from minds of men,
Whose fear and hope reach out beyond their ken.

10.

When I no more can stir my soul to move,
And life is but the ashes of a fire;
When I can but remember that my heart
Once used to live and love, long and aspire, –
Oh, be thou then the first, the one thou art;
Be thou the calling, before all answering love,
And in me wake hope, fear, boundless desire.

11.

I thought that I had lost thee; but, behold!
Thou comest to me from the horizon low,
Across the fields outspread of green and gold –
Fair carpet for thy feet to come and go.
Whence I know not, or how to me thou art come! –
Not less my spirit with calm bliss doth glow,
Meeting thee only thus, in nature vague and dumb.

1/8

To pray without ceasing – the Jesus prayer –
My heart beats momently within God's grace;
No flint but gentlest touch recalls love's fire;
The spellbound converse lights the silent sayer
Beyond reminders, goad, rote. Mercy's place
In everything we see, smell, touch, breathe – air!
Inhale to lift the veil of heavenly lace.

1/9

Lost out here in the stars or truly found –
Orphan in an empty dream or next-of-Kin?
Spot-intervention or heart's life within?
Faith is not blind, and yours, George, is renowned!
Yet as you work these poems out, sound by sound,
We get them in your future, rich and deep –
Knowing in Him, you slumber not nor sleep.

1/10

This is the prayer-exact I pray today,
My loves and dreams cremated in a homely urn;
Heart just as frozen as a wintry log
That only splits but will not rightly burn.
Call even me, Lord, through this mournful fog:
Love me, awaken me, so that I may
Crack in the grave-crust: love and bloom and turn!

1/11

Yes, in a certain color of the sky,
At dawn and dusk (lavender-apricot)
Mystical consolations do abide,
And into that benign and subtle sigh –
All of the bitter sorrows distant ride.
In emptiness, with one forget-me-not
Pressed in a book, I seek shells at low tide.

12.

Doubt swells and surges, with swelling doubt behind!
My soul in storm is but a tattered sail,
Streaming its ribbons on the torrent gale;
In calm, 'tis but a limp and flapping thing:
Oh! swell it with thy breath; make it a wing, –
To sweep through thee the ocean, with thee the wind
Nor rest until in thee its haven it shall find.

13.

The idle flapping of the sail is doubt;
Faith swells it full to breast the breasting seas.
Bold, conscience, fast, and rule the ruling helm;
Hell's freezing north no tempest can send out,
But it shall toss thee homeward to thy leas;
Boisterous wave-crest never shall o'erwhelm
Thy sea-float bark as safe as field-borne rooted elm.

14.

Sometimes, hard-trying, it seems I cannot pray –
For doubt, and pain, and anger, and all strife.
Yet some poor half-fledged prayer-bird from the nest
May fall, flit, fly, perch – crouch in the bowery breast
Of the large, nation-healing tree of life; –
Moveless there sit through all the burning day,
And on my heart at night a fresh leaf cooling lay.

15.

My harvest withers. Health, my means to live –
All things seem rushing straight into the dark.
But the dark still is God. I would not give
The smallest silver-piece to turn the rush
Backward or sideways. Am I not a spark
Of him who is the light? – Fair hope doth flush
My east. – Divine success – Oh, hush and hark!

1/12

I cannot pray a prayer so vast as this!
A timid rower in a paper boat –
In such a storm of doubt I cannot float
Yet am most deaf to forces of nay-sayers,
Trusting you'll fish me out, read my wet prayers,
Unfold my boat within your awesome bliss
And save me from the chaos with a kiss.

1/13

Outnumbered by official public words
Proclaiming lovely truths that are pat lies,
I float my little rowboat without oars
Alone, and far from convivial shores.
Sometimes the *V* of migratory birds
Heartens me, sometimes a shining fish flies
Over my head in snowy, frozen skies.

1/14

I do not try – he deepens more in me
With every day I am swept by his stream
Down, down the cold calendar of the days
In frozen reflecting ice, in white, free
Plumes of promise; every moment I dream
Past death/aridity: "Create in me
A clean heart, O Lord – let me be like thee."

1/15

From your precarity we harvest now!
The planet tilts upon the edge of fear.
Within this healing tree, each holy bough...
In Godly darkness now we pray and trust –
As your bright ember lights this frozen year,
We rise in hope from sorrows' tearstained dust
To see thy promised dawn – are still – and hear!

16.

Thy will be done. I yield up everything.
"The life is more than meat" – then more than health;
"The body more than raiment"– then than wealth;
The hairs I made not, thou art numbering.
Thou art my life – I the brook, thou the spring.
Because thine eyes are open, I can see;
Because thou art thyself, 'tis therefore I am me.

17.

No sickness can come near to blast my health;
My life depends not upon any meat;
My bread comes not from any human tilth;
No wings will grow upon my changeless wealth;
Wrong cannot touch it, violence or deceit;
Thou art my life, my health, my bank, my barn –
And from all other gods thou plain dost warn.

18.

Care thou for mine whom I must leave behind;
Care that they know who 'tis for them takes care;
Thy present patience help them still to bear;
Lord, keep them clearing, growing, heart and mind;
In one thy oneness us together bind;
Last earthly prayer with which to thee I cling –
Grant that, save love, we owe not anything.

19.

'Tis well, for unembodied thought a live,
True house to build – of stubble, wood, nor hay;
So, like bees round the flower by which they thrive,
My thoughts are busy with the informing truth,
And as I build, I feed, and grow in youth –
Hoping to stand fresh, clean, and strong, and gay,
When up the east comes dawning His great day.

1/16

Amen! As George does, Lord, so we do too.
O, may we stream into MacDonald's brook;
That mindful of you in this mirror-book,
We realize with keenness freshly new –
Through, with, and in you we receive life true:
'Tis you yourself look through our mortal eyes –
And every day, your bread, we grateful rise!

1/17

The northwest wind, snow flea-small flying bright,
Narcissus buds in cobalt measuring cup,
Pink dawn, on radio, names of war-dead,
From each rooftop, smoke-prayers puffing up
And out into the changeless, brilliant light;
Now I understand what is meant by bread
And roses – work and love, blood-red, hope-white.

1/18

I listen here outside the church, my heart
Peeled like a green apple as I forget
Myself. See that old face of sorrow? Cue
The rewind, all the way back to the start.
I leave behind some images, some art;
Debris of treasure, questions and regret.
My line is ended – faith itself brand-new.

1/19

I stand in the true house your thoughts have raised,
Protected by these strong-hewn poems of faith.
This morn' my unembodied thoughts are dazed.
I need to form a candle from your hive,
And by its light become once more alive.
God made the world in seven days; this eighth,
May he create a person from a wraith.

20.

Thy will is truth — 'tis therefore fate, the strong.
Would that my will did sweep full swing with thine!
Then harmony with every spheric song,
And conscious power, would give sureness divine.
Who thinks to thread thy great laws' onward throng,
Is as a fly that creeps his foolish way
Athwart an engine's wheels in smooth resistless play.

21.

Thou in my heart hast planted, gardener divine,
A scion of the tree of life: it grows;
But not in every wind or weather it blows;
The leaves fall sometimes from the baby tree,
And the life-power seems melting into pine;
Yet still the sap keeps struggling to the shine,
And the unseen root clings cramplike unto thee.

22.

Do thou, my God, my spirit's weather control;
And as I do not gloom though the day be dun,
Let me not gloom when earth-born vapours roll
Across the infinite zenith of my soul.
Should sudden brain-frost through the heart's summer run,
Cold, weary, joyless, waste of air and sun,
Thou art my south, my summer-wind, my all, my one.

23.

O Life, why dost thou close me up in death?
O Health, why make me inhabit heaviness? —
I ask, yet know: the sum of this distress,
Pang-haunted body, sore-dismayed mind,
Is but the egg that rounds the winged faith;
When that its path into the air shall find,
My heart will follow, high above cold, rain, and wind.

1/20

I do not know thy will, I only know
I want to be one with it. Teach me more,
Please, or trust me to bumble by degrees
Upon the straight and narrow on my knees,
Or balancing upon the tightrope, so
High I can commune with none but thee; war
Just distant folly on the circus floor.

1/21

My little scion, fiercely pruned, still lives.
The ancient blood cements the holy bond
As prismed light-chips on the frozen pond
Spark heaven's grace in this old grafted bud.
Deep in the coldframe your assurance gives:
No longer shall I set to sea in sieves,
But do your will and grow in snow or mud.

1/22

The glimmer-light of God herein is hope;
Such love within warms every icy scene.
The gratitudes for food, clothes, shelter sing
Within the snowstorm as bright birds take wing.
A piano on the radio sends green
Rhymes. I dance, raising an icicle-trope-
Unicorn-horn sceptre, as though a queen.

1/23

Each year is like a day, each day a year.
The egg is cracked, the wind is cold and clear.
The feathers of love's warm breast brood until
Newbeing is accustomed to the chill.
It is intensely real, sad and sweet.
The present tense is infinite retreat –
A mobius where earth and heaven meet.

24.

I can no more than lift my weary eyes;
Therefore I lift my weary eyes – no more.
But my eyes pull my heart, and that, before
'Tis well awake, knocks where the conscience lies;
Conscience runs quick to the spirit's hidden door:
Straightway, from every sky-ward window, cries
Up to the Father's listening ears arise.

25.

Not in my fancy now I search to find thee;
Not in its loftiest forms would shape or bind thee;
I cry to one whom I can never know,
Filling me with an infinite overflow;
Not to a shape that dwells within my heart,
Clothed in perfections love and truth assigned thee,
But to the God thou knowest that thou art.

26.

Not, Lord, because I have done well or ill;
Not that my mind looks up to thee clear-eyed;
Not that it struggles in fast cerements tied;
Not that I need thee daily sorer still;
Not that I, wretched, wander from thy will;
Not now for any cause to thee I cry,
But this, that thou art thou, and here am I.

27.

Yestereve, Death came, and knocked at my thin door.
I from my window looked: the thing I saw,
The shape uncouth, I had not seen before.
I was disturbed – with fear, in sooth, not awe;
Whereof ashamed, I instantly did rouse
My will to seek thee – only to fear the more:
Alas! I could not find thee in the house.

1/24

You do so well to tell us that the small
Hope, glance, intention – is at times
The only little bell we have that chimes.
Eyes, heart and conscience, spirit, profound call –
All linked and threading through these daily rhymes –
God hears and takes and breaks (as bread) our all;
Infinitesmal manna from the Fall.

1/25

Fatherless, I find thee, Jesus, brother –
Turn to Mary, from my own earth-mother;
Say the 'Our Father', pray to the unknown,
Seeking the Most High who wills me, alone,
Through crusts and constructs, up from my own grave.
Even me – bone-dry, ignorant, *other* –
Thy overflowing mercy cares to save.

1/26

Not, Lord, because I fail to stay in tune;
Not that I tremble in my burial shroud;
Not that I pray in truth with my head bowed,
Not that I want more than this winter moon;
Not that I fall silent, or sing, or cry;
Not that I mirror hope, or aim too high,
But this, that you love, ergo so may I.

1/27

Strong Death bides time outside my mother's door.
Her sturdy cheer is beautiful to see.
Both lonely and a celebrant she cleaves
To music; never will believe in "thee".
Forsaken, isolate, her daughter grieves
The poignant battles of this little war –
Rejoicing that the love is evermore!

28.

I was like Peter when he began to sink.
To thee a new prayer therefore I have got –
That, when Death comes in earnest to my door,
Thou wouldst thyself go, when the latch doth clink,
And lead him to my room, up to my cot;
Then hold thy child's hand, hold and leave him not,
Till Death has done with him for evermore.

29.

Till Death has done with him? – Ah, leave me then!
And Death has done with me, oh, nevermore!
He comes – and goes – to leave me in thy arms,
Nearer thy heart, oh, nearer than before!
To lay thy child, naked, new-born again
Of mother earth, crept free through many harms,
Upon thy bosom – still to the very core.

30.

Come to me, Lord: I will not speculate how,
Nor think at which door I would have thee appear,
Nor put off calling till my floors be swept,
But cry, "Come, Lord, come any way, come now."
Doors, windows, I throw wide; my head I bow,
And sit like some one who so long has slept
That he knows nothing till his life draw near.

31.

O Lord, I have been talking to the people;
Thought's wheels have round me whirled a fiery zone,
And the recoil of my words' airy ripple
My heart unheedful has puffed up and blown.
Therefore I cast myself before thee prone:
Lay cool hands on my burning brain, and press
From my weak heart the swelling emptiness.

1/28

Father, I don't dare ask you for your touch;
Nor that you'd be with me when your midwife
Arrives to free me through the dreadful grave.
That would seem a kindly mercy too much
Beyond imagining. You gave me life.
My sorry failures cut me like a knife.
Here is my one-word prayer, always: *Save!*

1/29

Once in a nightmare that was madness real,
Escaping one who beat me yellow-blue,
I pressed my mouth against the breast of earth,
Ran naked over corn-stubble, *free!* Few
Who cross that border return; the wind's feel
On my face, sure death, and the long, slow birth
Into sane childhood – by grace – with shy zeal.

1/30

You fear Death, fear the absence of God more.
Deaths were my foundlings; I lived on grief,
A spinster, carding poems upon the floor;
But at their graves found prelude to belief.
Though God is yet a morsel in my heart –
My heart a barnwood coop with broken door –
You sweep me clean and empty by your art.

1/31

Last day of the first month of the new year:
I build an icicle tower/steeple
For the birds, that I may hopefully say
I am not your dull girl, all work no play.
Help me, as I go among your people,
To watch and listen lovingly, give ear
In real communion – learn from all I hear.

FEBRUARY.

1.

I to myself have neither power nor worth,
Patience nor love, nor anything right good;
My soul is a poor land, plenteous in dearth –
Here blades of grass, there a small herb for food –
A nothing that would be something if it could;
But if obedience, Lord, in me do grow,
I shall one day be better than I know.

2.

The worst power of an evil mood is this –
It makes the bastard self seem in the right,
Self, self the end, the goal of human bliss.
But if the Christ-self in us be the might
Of saving God, why should I spend my force
With a dark thing to reason of the light –
Not push it rough aside, and hold obedient course?

3.

Back still it comes to this: there was a man
Who said, "I am the truth, the life, the way:" –
Shall I pass on, or shall I stop and hear? –
"Come to the Father but by me none can:"
What then is this? – am I not also one
Of those who live in fatherless dismay?
I stand, I look, I listen, I draw near.

FEBRUARY

2/1

Nothing on my soul-land but one small bird,
And three cracked-corn grains by the still waters.
February (from *februum*, Sabine word
For *means of purification* – daughters
Raped, conquered and absorbed by Roman force).
Though Rachel, inconsolable, now weeps,
Nazarene branch is budding in the deeps.

2/2

Two/two: white swans that glide as church bells toll,
Toxic debris floats down on East Texas.
Two, the imposter and the Christ-child soul,
War-spin split-screen of the tv nexus.
Each jet tremor echoes: nine/eleven –
Two goes 'round, comes 'round the twin-towers hole,
As "homeland" is coined/bent to mean "heaven".

2/3

I draw near to you who made, in the dark,
David's star shine on immortal water –
Father Son Spirit / Mother Soul Daughter –
United trinities, brilliant as One,
Mystical fusion of moon and the sun,
Calming the currents that lift Noah's ark,
Keeping alight Easter's Holy Fire spark!

4.

My Lord, I find that nothing else will do,
But follow where thou goest, sit at thy feet,
And where I have thee not, still run to meet.
Roses are scentless, hopeless are the morns,
Rest is but weakness, laughter crackling thorns,
If thou, the Truth, do not make them the true:
Thou art my life, O Christ, and nothing else will do.

5.

Thou art here – in heaven, I know, but not *from* here –
Although thy separate self do not appear;
If I could part the light from out the day,
There I should have thee! But thou art too near:
How find thee walking, when thou art the way?
Oh, present Christ! make my eyes keen as stings,
To see thee at their heart, the glory even of things.

6.

That thou art nowhere to be found, agree
Wise men, whose eyes are but for surfaces;
Men with eyes opened by the second birth,
To whom the seen, husk of the unseen is,
Descry thee soul of everything on earth.
Who know thy ends, thy means and motions see:
Eyes made for glory soon discover thee.

7.

Thou near then, I draw nearer – to thy feet,
And sitting in thy shadow, look out on the shine;
Ready at thy first word to leave my seat –
Not you: thou goest too. From every clod
Into thy footprint flows the indwelling wine;
And in my daily bread, keen-eyed I greet
Its being's heart, the very body of God.

2/4

Stronger than science, Lord, and sweet as rain,
Through hi-tech toys and candles of the poor,
Here at your feet, with Mary we may moor.
Finding from all four corners of thy cross,
Gifts to illumine every earthly loss;
Here we *do nothing* – bearing grief, loss, pain –
Crucified, wed, sealed with a kiss, like Cain.

2/5

Lord, I am sad, encompassed 'round by fear –
Your little world seems on its funeral bier.
I must discern you in the gathering dark,
Both rest in peace, and rise within you here.
As a true mourner, bearing Cain's own mark,
Give me good ears to hear you when I pray,
And let me know you in the tasks of day.

2/6

As sleet bombards the icy, lonely place –
Infinitesmal breath, thought, gesture, word,
Wise hope (best visible when slow as peace),
Small task – sends loving gratitudes unseen
Through galaxies in melodies unheard.
We black sheep offer you, dear Lord, our fleece;
You keep us everwarm in unearned grace!

2/7

Your Eucharist in every nourishment,
Your body and your blood in everything,
Your holy name invoked in soldiers' tent,
And in our homes as we await sure death;
The prophet's warning and the pebble's ring,
Here in the time of perpetual Lent –
Help me, dear Lord – I cannot get my breath!

8.

Thou wilt interpret life to me, and men,
Art, nature, yea, my own soul's mysteries –
Bringing truth out, clear-joyous, to my ken,
Fair as the morn trampling the dull night. Then
The lone hill-side shall hear exultant cries;
The joyous see me joy, the weeping weep;
The watching smile, as Death breathes on me his cold sleep.

9.

I search my heart – I search, and find no faith.
Hidden He may be in its many folds –
I see him not revealed in all the world
Duty's firm shape thins to a misty wraith.
No good seems likely. To and fro I am hurled.
I have no stay. Only obedience holds: –
I haste, I rise, I do the thing he saith.

10.

Thou wouldst not have thy man crushed back to clay;
It must be, God, thou hast a strength to give
To him that fain would do what thou dost say;
Else how shall any soul repentant live,
Old griefs and new fears hurrying on dismay?
Let pain be what thou wilt, kind and degree,
Only in pain calm thou my heart with thee.

11.

I will not shift my ground like Moab's king,
But from this spot whereon I stand, I pray –
From this same barren rock to thee I say,
"Lord, in my commonness, in this very thing
That haunts my soul with folly – through the clay
Of this my pitcher, see the lamp's dim flake;
And hear the blow that would the pitcher break."

2/8

As nourishment revives the mood and sight,
As outer harvests mulch interior
Blossom – we grow old and up! we grow up! –
So does the scythe of death restore the cup
As salvation, show the world *maya* bright.
Slain in the Spirit, husk inferior,
Buried/brand new, we rise into the light.

2/9

If life and faith were flat, a hollow boat,
Ourselves but cardboard characters, thin-skinned,
We would surrender to the scissors sharp,
Quash poppycock of godbliss/angelharp.
Aground at low tide, how could we set sail?
Obedience is bubble in that wind,
Reminding us it's empty things that float

2/10

My heart's in no way calm within this pain,
But pulverized, as when a tilted pot
On your wheel asks to be made right as rain;
Cut from the bat, returned to clay; all hot
Thoughts quenched, sliced, kneaded, centered, all to gain:
I am a lump, Lord, dreaming of a cup –
Put your palms on my new heart – draw me up!

2/11

I cannot even stand my ground, just sit;
My lungs are sick, the dog is too; a stone
Makes fractures in this daft clay bell; alone,
I fled the city. Fifty ducks now, lit
In sun-snow, war news, anguish in the bone.
All light is yours, Lord. My prayers are tears –
I love you and am broken by these fears.

12.

Be thou the well by which I lie and rest;
Be thou my tree of life, my garden ground;
Be thou my home, my fire, my chamber blest,
My book of wisdom, loved of all the best;
Oh, be my friend, each day still newer found,
As the eternal days and nights go round!
Nay, nay – thou art *my God*, in whom all loves are bound!

13.

Two things at once, thou know'st I cannot think.
When busy with the work thou givest me,
I cannot consciously think then of thee.
Then why, when next thou lookest o'er the brink
Of my horizon, should my spirit shrink,
Reproached and fearful, nor to greet thee run?
Can I be two when I am only one!

14.

My soul must unawares have sunk awry.
Some care, poor eagerness, ambition of work,
Some old offence that unforgiving did lurk,
Or some self-gratulation, soft and sly –
Something not thy sweet will, not the good part,
While the home-guard looked out, stirred up the old murk,
And so I gloomed away from thee, my Heart.

15.

Therefore I make provision, ere I begin
To do the thing thou givest me to do,
Praying, – Lord, wake me oftener, lest I sin.
Amidst my work, open thine eyes on me,
That I may wake and laugh, and know and see
Then with healed heart afresh catch up the clue,
And singing drop into my work anew.

2/12

Be thou the word engendering wisdom's seed;
Be thou the prayer – illuminate my heart;
Be thou the solace in the widow's weed,
Be thou the life in liturgy and creed;
Though stunned, in awe, we stumble at the start,
Come near, Dear, please, to us who (set apart)
Long to repay thy myriad gifts in art.

2/13

Two things at once (and more) I often think;
My parents split, and made me letter *Y*.
Doubleness and division are my sky.
Will you, my root/task/prayer/sap/word – ink –
Sweet dawning of the day in baby pink,
Beget me, dying, budded, bruiséd reed,
That *I* may bloom in oneness, wand and seed?

2/14

Assailed by imperfections, I still call –
Sweeping the house while yet most sick from dust –
For your kind mercy which redeems my trust.
My fossilized resentments crack and fall.
A gifted brother on his death-bed lies,
He served you, lived in love and music; must
I release him? Can "let go" mean he dies?

2/15

We sinners whose awakening was rude,
At edge of precipice, at childhood's end –
Must quell downright astonishment to hear
An invitation to a realm past fear.
What, sing? You mean God's eye is on the friend,
And on the sparrow, and on me? Saint Jude!
Impossible forgiveness – mystic food!

16.

If I should slow diverge, and listless stray
Into some thought, feeling, or dream unright,
O Watcher, my backsliding soul affray;
Let me not perish of the ghastly blight.
Be thou, O Life eternal, in me light;
Then merest approach of selfish or impure
Shall start me up alive, awake, secure.

17.

Lord, I have fallen again – a human clod!
Selfish I was, and heedless to offend;
Stood on my rights. Thy own child would not send
Away his shreds of nothing for the whole God!
Wretched, to thee who savest, low I bend:
Give me the power to let my rag-rights go
In the great wind that from thy gulf doth blow.

18.

Keep me from wrath, let it seem ever so right:
My wrath will never work thy righteousness.
Up, up the hill, to the whiter than snow-shine,
Help me to climb, and dwell in pardon's light.
I must be pure as thou, or ever less
Than thy design of me – therefore incline
My heart to take men's wrongs as thou tak'st mine.

19.

Lord, in thy spirit's hurricane, I pray,
Strip my soul naked – dress it then thy way.
Change for me all my rags to cloth of gold.
Who would not poverty for riches yield?
A hovel sell to buy a treasure-field?
Who would a mess of porridge careful hold
Against the universe's birthright old?

2/16

Like pintail duck and last bright grain of corn,
I waddle on the ice to marvel how –
Though solitaire within the icy morn
Reflected in the frozen pond just now –
Your tender mercy shines like kernel vow
Within the lantern soul in Sunday light;
Emmaus bread breaks; so does day from night!

2/17

Tried to collect old letters as though eggs,
All day on cyber goose-chase and no dice;
Meanwhile the ducks snow-covered on the ice
Swim on, pumping their cold bright orange legs;
While I, too conscious of my every vice,
Bless you who shroud our plans in saving snow,
And lift our frozen ark from tides of woe!

2/18

My wrath and fear are two sides of a stone
Kept in a dark cave to make sure I'm strong;
These are the dreams of a sleeping black bear.
May I now these besetting sins disown,
Without projecting on others my wrong.
Call me, dear Lord, from the penitent's lair,
To shed my old skin, and climb thy bright stair.

2/19

Something within says, "do not reach too high,
You are not worthy," and you well know why.
Give me for soup your bowl of milky way.
Transform/make me good – sackcloth will be fine.
Clothe me in mercy; may I know it mine.
If it be thy will, Lord, help me to fast –
So that heaven's needle-eye will seem vast.

20.

Help me to yield my will, in labour even,
Nor toil on toil, greedy of doing, heap –
Fretting I cannot more than me is given;
That with the finest clay my wheel runs slow,
Nor lets the lovely thing the shapely grow;
That memory what thought gives it cannot keep,
And nightly rimes ere morn like cistus-petals go.

21.

'Tis – shall thy will be done for me? – or mine,
And I be made a thing not after thine –
My own, and dear in paltriest details?
Shall I be born of God, or of mere man?
Be made like Christ, or on some other plan? –
I let all run: – set thou and trim my sails;
Home then my course, let blow whatever gales.

22.

With thee on board, each sailor is a king
Nor I mere captain of my vessel then,
But heir of earth and heaven, eternal child;
Daring all truth, nor fearing anything;
Mighty in love, the servant of all men;
Resenting nothing, taking rage and blare
Into the Godlike silence of a loving care.

23.

I cannot see, my God, a reason why
From morn to night I go not gladsome free;
For, if thou art what my soul thinketh thee,
There is no burden but should lightly lie,
No duty but a joy at heart must be:
Love's perfect will can be nor sore nor small,
For God is light – in him no darkness is at all.

2/20

Rock roses red in supermarkets know
My thoughts disperse like dandelion lawn-
Weed seedling snow-globes on timeless tides; blow
Drifting past unpublished words, unfinished
Art, lost parts; thy gifts in me diminished
Just as small confidence begins to dawn;
May I not *build*, Lord – may I only *grow*!

2/21

Oh, let me know thy will and hear it well,
Discerning self from sooth here in the cell
Of cowardice, confusion; so unsure
I act not, lest my motives be impure.
Let thy small voice be compass, living God,
That led by grace and thy divining rod,
I'll root, threshed from the husk – arise from sod.

2/22

I sail as though a mermaid cabin-child,
Part-stowaway, within the golden barque
"Precarity," an old boat made of loss;
The sails are edged in great-price pearls and moss.
Sometimes I row on in the quiet dark
With oars forgiveness/trust; sometimes the wild
Gales rage – the only starlight is Cain's mark!

2/23

This is acceptance – hopeful heart and head –
Which says it all, regarding trust and cheer.
Even imperfect love can cast out fear!
George speaks of duty – that we must from dead
Despair and "why me?" tombs rise up and hear
That your great good by tender alchemy,
Re-creates us: new beings, glad and free.

24.

'Tis something thus to think, and half to trust –
But, ah! my very heart, God-born, should lie
Spread to the light, clean, clear of mire and rust,
And like a sponge drink the divine sunbeams.
What resolution then, strong, swift, and high!
What pure devotion, or to live or die!
And in my sleep, what true, what perfect dreams!

25.

There is a misty twilight of the soul,
A sickly eclipse, low brooding o'er a man,
When the poor brain is as an empty bowl,
And the thought-spirit, weariful and wan,
Turning from that which yet it loves the best,
Sinks moveless, with life-poverty opprest: –
Watch then, O Lord, thy feebly glimmering coal.

26.

I cannot think; in me is but a void;
I have felt much, and want to feel no more;
My soul is hungry for some poorer fare –
Some earthly nectar, gold not unalloyed: –
The little child that's happy to the core,
Will leave his mother's lap, run down the stair,
Play with the servants – is his mother annoyed?

27.

I would not have it so. Weary and worn,
Why not to thee run straight, and be at rest?
Motherward, with toy new, or garment torn,
The child that late forsook her changeless breast,
Runs to home's heart, the heaven that's heavenliest:
In joy or sorrow, feebleness or might,
Peace or commotion, be thou, Father, my delight.

2/24

Love – love alone will break the secret code;
Anchorite-vagabonds, both hives and bees;
Eternally displaced persons who root,
Cannot always believe they're bearing fruit.
Christ breaks off wheat-buds on the pilgrim road
Of Sabbath, scripture in the streaming breeze –
Sifting the truth until it salts the seas.

2/25

One smouldering twig in cold stove was my part;
Last night you fanned it with a wild, absurd
Delivery man (breath of Cupid's dart)
Who fixed the furnace and with one kind word
Disturbed and tempted all that is stone cold;
Danced in the snow! Just as I feel so old –
Joy's messenger brings fire to my heart.

2/26

Sometimes a servant has more love than kin;
Possessive love is not the sweetest kind.
Pewter and brass are lovely; water is
Bliss to thirst, even in a cup of tin.
This little child, happy as thoughts unwind,
Plays with Jesus, knowing her love is his;
Her mother, jealous, sighs but does not sin.

2/27

Long fatherless, I never learned to trust;
Seldom rested, guarded the home latchkey,
Tried to be brave while scared, evading lust.
I cannot run to thee, I live in thee.
Today a genius brother is stardust.
I bow, our Father, in the dawn's snowlight,
Under the Mercy, pray you bless his flight.

28.

The thing I would say, still comes forth with doubt
And difference: – is it that thou shap'st my ends?
Or is it only the necessity
Of stubborn words, that shift sluggish about,
Warping my thought as it the sentence bends? –
Have thou a part in it, O Lord, and I
Shall say a truth, if not the thing I try.

29.

Gather my broken fragments to a whole,
As these four quarters make a shining day.
Into thy basket, for my golden bowl,
Take up the things that I have cast away
In vice or indolence or unwise play.
Let mine be a merry, all-receiving heart,
But make it a whole, with light in every part.

2/28

Amen! How well I know the fusion of
Intention/inspiration; may thy word
Here shape, surprise and lead my every look
In clarity, in meditation, love –
Ascend like David's white, free, holy bird –
Scattering constructs by the freshet brook
Found by thy bending green-twig shepherd's crook.

2/29

Make me a *pique-assiette* heart; with each shard
Imprinted by your sweet, abiding love.
Though being pulverized was mighty hard,
May new heart be the chalice, spirit-dove.
May tempests in such teacups be benign,
Transfigured sins become the Host divine,
And shining mercies be the outward sign.

MARCH.

1.

THE song birds that come to me night and morn,
Fly oft away and vanish if I sleep,
Nor to my fowling-net will one return:
Is the thing ever ours we cannot keep? –
But their souls go not out into the deep.
What matter if with changed song they come back?
Old strength nor yet fresh beauty shall they lack.

2.

Gloriously wasteful, O my Lord, art thou!
Sunset faints after sunset into the night,
Splendorously dying from thy window-sill –
For ever. Sad our poverty doth bow
Before the riches of thy making might:
Sweep from thy space thy systems at thy will –
In thee the sun sets every sunset still.

3.

And in the perfect time, O perfect God,
When we are in our home, our natal home,
When joy shall carry every sacred load,
And from its life and peace no heart shall roam,
What if thou make us able to make like thee –
To light with moons, to clothe with greenery,
To hang gold sunsets o'er a rose and purple sea!

MARCH

3/1

How can I lose that which I never had?
Deeper the loss the more the man is "mine".
Those who most hurt me I must love the best.
What a paradoxical valentine!
The more I let go, the more I may hold;
Grief fills the golden bowl with holy tears;
Joy makes a home in hope beyond all fears.

3/2

An only child, born rich, with talents rife –
He cultivated these gifts all his life.
Now in the stone house "Given" your seed lies.
We sing "For All Thy Saints", the widow cries.
Help us believe the harvest splits the stone,
That he in forgiveness is truly sown,
And face-to-face now, loved and dearly known!

3/3

This world's a play, players, when you are free.
While you are lighting lights, apprenticing,
I must remember glorious earth as womb.
Oft have I seen thy firstborns split the tomb.
When I'm reborn in death I hope I sing
A nervous little tendril tune to thee,
That, surrendered, I too may bloom and be!

4.

Then to his neighbour one may call out, "Come!
Brother, come hither – I would show you a thing;"
And lo, a vision of his imagining,
Informed of thought which else had rested dumb,
Before the neighbour's truth-delighted eyes,
In the great æther of existence rise,
And two hearts each to each the closer cling!

5.

We make, but thou art the creating core.
Whatever thing I dream, invent, or feel,
Thou art the heart of it, the atmosphere.
Thou art inside all love man ever bore;
Yea, the love itself, whatever thing be dear.
Man calls his dog, he follows at his heel,
Because thou first art love, self-caused, essential, mere.

6.

This day be with me, Lord, when I go forth,
Be nearer to me than I am able to ask.
In merriment, in converse, or in task,
Walking the street, listening to men of worth,
Or greeting such as only talk and bask,
Be thy thought still my waiting soul around,
And if He come, I shall be watching found.

7.

What if, writing, I always seem to leave
Some better thing, or better way, behind,
Why should I therefore fret at all, or grieve!
The worse I drop, that I the better find;
The best is only in thy perfect mind.
Fallen threads I will not search for – I will weave.
Who makes the mill-wheel backward strike to grind!

3/4

When Psyche's sisters saw Love's palace bright,
Wonder and envy fought; green envy won.
They left her candle, knife, doubt, poison fears.
When she saw his perfection in such light,
He woke and vanished. She, a beggar-nun,
Wandered beyond negation's bogus night
Into the bliss one finds through holy tears.

3/5

As the umbilical is cut, oh Lord,
Teach me the alphabet from A to Z.
I call my dog – she does not always come,
Nor does she heel; I keep her on a cord.
Teach me to follow; newly create me
Tame and loving, keen to catch each bright crumb
That falls from the table; then set me free.

3/6

Saint Teresa said, "*If you are willing*
To bear the trial of being displeasing
To yourself, then you will be for Jesus
A pleasant place of shelter." This filling
Lenten crumb sustains me, somewhat easing
Penitential anguish on my knees. Fuss
Not. Pray. Await the Bridegroom every day.

3/7

I do not know what thy will is for me –
So many gifts there are to cultivate;
I walk on words, as painting calls, and song!
My mind's a crazy quilt; each idea, great
And small, a harlequin, and I must wait.
Center my heart in thee that I may be
And know; discern your leading, soon or late.

8.

Be with me, Lord. Keep me beyond all prayers:
For more than all my prayers my need of thee,
And thou beyond all need, all unknown cares;
What the heart's dear imagination dares,
Thou dost transcend in measureless majesty
All prayers in one – my God, be unto me
Thy own eternal self, absolutely.

9.

Where should the unknown treasures of the truth
Lie, but there whence the truth comes out the most –
In the Son of man, folded in love and ruth?
Fair shore we see, fair ocean; but behind
Lie infinite reaches bathing many a coast –
The human thought of the eternal mind,
Pulsed by a living tide, blown by a living wind.

10.

Thou, healthful Father, art the Ancient of Days,
And Jesus is the eternal youth of thee.
Our old age is the scorching of the bush
By life's indwelling, incorruptible blaze.
O Life, burn at this feeble shell of me,
Till I the sore singed garment off shall push,
Flap out my Psyche wings, and to thee rush.

11.

But shall I then rush to thee like a dart?
Or lie long hours æonian yet betwixt
This hunger in me, and the Father's heart? –
It shall be good, how ever, and not ill;
Of things and thoughts even now thou art my next;
Sole neighbour, and no space between, thou art –
And yet art drawing nearer, nearer still.

3/8

Within the dandelion orb of seed,
May I be thee-anchored, and ready too
To float on merest spirit breath (*I am*)
Into the ethers of the pascal lamb.
However phantoms shadow/spin my view,
Your loving peace comforts my every need:
Grace in the greenhouse rose/the roadside weed.

3/9

Oceans of grief, soldiers in dust storms;
Obdurate powers, military men.
Quicksands of longing, duty; ill thought-forms,
Calcified fears and hatreds never cease.
All sides cry, "Truth!" and dip the bloody pen
In martyr's veins, seeking the sweet release
Death brings within the dream of holy peace!

3/10

Some days I smell the charnel house within,
The smouldering holocaust of wartime days.
My birth among these victims sears me still;
I carry with me all these unknown kin
And hope to be their intercessor; gaze
At thy moon and stars, drinking my fill –
Grandiose, small – seeking thy triune will.

3/11

When I draw the arrow back to my ear
As far as I can, feather at my eye –
I myself am the prey. When I let go,
Force of the distance undermines my foe.
Targeting sin, the shaft finds, by and by
Its mark within and shears the husk so drear
From the blessed, faithful, thee-binding tie.

12.

Therefore, my brothers, therefore, sisters dear,
However I, troubled or selfish, fail
In tenderness, or grace, or service clear,
I every moment draw to you more near;
God in us from our hearts veil after veil
Keeps lifting, till we see with his own sight,
And all together run in unity's delight.

13.

I love thee, Lord, for very greed of love —
Not of the precious streams that towards me move,
But of the indwelling, outgoing, fountain store.
Than mine, oh, many an ignorant heart loves more!
Therefore the more, with Mary at thy feet,
I must sit worshipping — that, in my core,
Thy words may fan to a flame the low primeval heat.

14.

Oh my beloved, gone to heaven from me!
I would be rich in love to heap you with love;
I long to love you, sweet ones, perfectly —
Like God, who sees no spanning vault above,
No earth below, and feels no circling air —
Infinitely, no boundary anywhere.
I am a beast until I love as God doth love.

15.

Ah, say not, 'tis but perfect self I want
But if it were, that self is fit to live
Whose perfectness is still itself to scant,
Which never longs to have, but still to give.
A self I must have, or not be at all:
Love, give me a self self-giving — or let me fall
To endless darkness back, and free me from life's thrall.

3/12

I am hurt, troubled and selfish; see, just
Now I offered firewood – the man took
A full cord – and I felt I couldn't trust
My motives. Was it loneliness and lust
That prompted my solicitude? What book
Will say? For this dim fool, what truth is left
To help distinguish between love and theft?

3/13

I love thee strictly from hunger, starving;
(Father, rotten wood awaits thy carving!)
Jealous, needy, wounded, crying to thee
With each wheezing, concertina breath: free
Me with thy truth, break this blind odd thought-shell;
Create me Mary as I ought to be,
Thine, whose pierced feet have led me out of hell.

3/14

I though a thistle long to be a beast,
That I may love devoutly as my pet,
Rather than making human souls my east,
Sticking and pricking until blood is let.
Teach me to love as dog, then woman true,
So may *agape*'s detached, gentle dew
Inspire/revivify all loves anew.

3/15

Lord, let me learn to receive, lest to give
May be itself a barrier to keep
My self (armored by good deeds) quite intact –
Afraid of burden-gratitudes, exact
Beans counted, while thy grace escapes the sieve
And rigid scale. Let me now dare to live,
To take and give true love within thy deep.

16.

"Back," said I! Whither back? How to the dark?
From no dark came I, but the depths of light;
From the sun-heart I came, of love a spark:
What should I do but love with all my might?
To die of love severe and pure and stark,
Were scarcely loss; to lord a loveless height –
That were a living death, damnation's positive night.

17.

But love is life. To die of love is then
The only pass to higher life than this.
All love is death to loving, living men;
All deaths are leaps across clefts to the abyss.
Our life is the broken current, Lord, of thine,
Flashing from morn to morn with conscious shine –
Then first by willing death self-made, then life divine.

18.

I love you, my sweet children, who are gone
Into another mansion; but I know
I love you not as I shall love you yet.
I love you, sweet dead children; there are none
In the land to which ye vanished to go,
Whose hearts more truly on your hearts are set –
Yet should I die of grief to love you only so.

19.

"I am but as a beast before thee, Lord." –
Great poet-king, I thank thee for the word. –
Leave not thy son half-made in beastly guise –
Less than a man, with more than human cries –
An unshaped thing in which thyself cries out!
Finish me, Father; now I am but a doubt;
Oh! make thy moaning thing for joy to leap and shout.

3/16

'Midst morning light, I sit by cybergleam;
In the radio chapel my heart-pleas
On ancient earth psalm-singers slowly stream.
Within, the silence of your lovely trees...
Who sing sublime as rooted as they seem.
Let me be true within your deepest seas,
Love – awaken me from this fearful dream.

3/17

The unrequited love is all I know
On earth, the *nothing lasts forever* kind.
Since even this is from your cupid's bow,
I come to archer-death, out of my mind,
Out of illusions, with a broken heart,
Leaving the gravecloths in the cave of art,
Seeking to join that of which I am part.

3/18

The sun is pink above snow-dusty trees.
I have no hope of seeing vanished two,
Yet I may mark their heavenly story
From the laundry room of purgatory,
Where faces print their winding sheets. The breeze
Of Holy Spirit melts snow-dust to dew,
'Till white sun, higher, warms dead hope anew.

3/19

On all fours, in a print by William Blake,
Thy daughter cries in anguish for the sake
Of endless wars, all murders, speech struck dumb.
Divinity and beast entwined, we come
Before thee, begging to be rightly made,
And by thy blood-streams deep be brave to wade,
Then rise in peace as frightened troops invade!

20.

Let my soul talk to thee in ordered words,
O king of kings, O lord of only lords! –
When I am thinking thee within my heart,
From the broken reflex be not far apart.
The troubled water, dim with upstirred soil,
Makes not the image which it yet can spoil: –
Come nearer, Lord, and smooth the wrinkled coil.

21.

O Lord, when I do think of my departed,
I think of thee who art the death of parting;
Of him who crying Father breathed his last,
Then radiant from the sepulchre upstarted. –
Even then, I think, thy hands and feet kept smarting:
With us the bitterness of death is past,
But by the feet he still doth hold us fast.

22.

Therefore our hands thy feet do hold as fast.
We pray not to be spared the sorest pang,
But only – be thou with us to the last.
Let not our heart be troubled at the clang
Of hammer and nails, nor dread the spear's keen fang,
Nor the ghast sickening that comes of pain,
Nor yet the last clutch of the banished brain.

23.

Lord, pity us: we have no making power;
Then give us making will, adopting thine.
Make, make, and make us; temper, and refine.
Be in us patience – neither to start nor cower.
Christ, if thou be not with us – not by sign,
But presence, actual as the wounds that bleed –
We shall not bear it, but shall die indeed.

3/20

Let my soul drift to thee on wordless breath,
O elder Brother, son of the Most High.
My brain, a winter stream, goes bubbling on,
From morning until night, from birth to death.
I, your brown duckling reverence you, Swan!
Sing, in your wake, a quackish lullabye,
Take up my pallet-splintered-wings and fly!

3/21

Now let our hands and feet be pierced as thine,
That every day the "habit of being"
Grows, reminding us in small, daily tasks
Which bind us to the cross, that we combine
Each doing with the knowing; that seeing
Into thy heart comes to each soul who asks –
Real life as precious blood in earthly casques.

3/22

I do not dare to hold thy feet, my Lord;
But venerate, and wash them with my tears,
And beg I be not cut off from that cord
That binds me to thy Marys (as their ears
Hear love, their eyes are raw with awful fears).
So, as my heart is cut by war's cold sword,
Through lenten floods, make me a place to ford!

3/23

No sooner taste thy presence; am assailed,
Fall, castigate myself in fury's tone...
The rage itself kills peace; I have twice failed.
May you in mercy have a funny-bone,
Because I have so next-to-nothing skill,
And hate myself so much I should be jailed,
And work so clownishly to do thy will.

24.

O Christ, have pity on all men when they come
Unto the border haunted of dismay;
When that they know not draweth very near –
The other thing, the opposite of day,
Formless and ghastly, sick, and gaping-dumb,
Before which even love doth lose his cheer:
O radiant Christ, remember then thy fear.

25.

Be by me, Lord, this day. Thou know'st I mean –
Lord, make me mind thee. I herewith forestall
My own forgetfulness, when I stoop to glean
The corn of earth – which yet thy hand lets fall.
Be for me then against myself. Oh lean
Over me then when I invert my cup;
Take me, if by the hair, and lift me up.

26.

Lord of essential life, help me to die.
To will to die is one with highest life,
The mightiest act that to Will's hand doth lie –
Born of God's essence, and of man's hard strife:
God, give me strength my evil self to kill,
And die into the heaven of thy pure will. –
Then shall this body's death be very tolerable.

27.

As to our mothers came help in our birth –
Not lost in lifing us, but saved and blest –
Self bearing self, although right sorely prest,
Shall nothing lose, but die and be at rest
In life eternal, beyond all care and dearth.
God-born then truly, a man does no more ill,
Perfectly loves, and has whate'er he will.

3/24

My father trembled so in fear, and I,
Not knowing how to comfort this stranger,
Shyly offered love, deep forgiveness; he,
Amidst his sense of impending danger,
Pressed my hand so dearly, and was to die
As I drove off. I thought I should be there!
Then someone said, "He wanted privacy."

3/25

As the sunlight falls on a broken chair,
As the muzak plays, masking war's young blood,
As the child's cries honk in the wild goose prayer,
As the snow-brooks stream through the earth's clay mud,
You lion-lamb breathe Jerusalem's air,
As our first-borns die, as we tremble here –
Come, Lord of bravest heart and smallest tear!

3/26

As the sun rises before the spring rain,
And spokesmen sell the war with peaceful words,
The demons play in my swept home; my Cain,
Domesticated, feeds the lovely birds...
My Abel prays his brother's love to win,
To be survivor in the rout of sin;
To die, thy mark a kiss upon my brow.

3/27

I have not time, between now and my life
In the vast dimensions beyond this one –
To be perfected; wrapped like a sham nun
In the shroud/placenta, far from thy sun,
Shamed by my sins, I try to be thy wife.
I cannot believe yet in thy heaven,
But hold fast to thy miracles seven.

28.

As our dear animals do suffer less
Because their pain spreads neither right nor left,
Lost in oblivion and foresightlessness –
Our suffering sore by faith shall be bereft
Of all dismay, and every weak excess.
His presence shall be better in our pain,
Than even self-absence to the weaker brain.

29.

"Father, let this cup pass." He prayed – was heard.
What cup was it that passed away from him?
Sure not the death-cup, now filled to the brim!
There was no quailing in the awful word;
He still was king of kings, of lords the lord: –
He feared lest, in the suffering waste and grim,
His faith might grow too faint and sickly dim.

30.

Thy mind, my master, I will dare explore;
What we are told, that we are meant to know.
Into thy soul I search yet more and more,
Led by the lamp of my desire and woe.
If thee, my Lord, I may not understand,
I am a wanderer in a houseless land,
A weeping thirst by hot winds ever fanned.

31.

Therefore I look again – and think I see
That, when at last he did cry out, "My God,
Why hast thou me forsaken?" straight man's rod
Was turned aside; for, that same moment, he
Cried "Father!" and gave up will and breath and spirit
Into his hands whose all he did inherit –
Delivered, glorified eternally.

3/28

This suffering – a flame that blacks bright fate
And pulverizes former forms to dust –
Warms frozen hearts afar we know not of.
Let me be like the mouse that my cat ate –
Eyes staring straight ahead, head off. The Just,
Beyond the law, past image/pearly gate –
Reside, not knowing what hit them, in Love.

3/29

When you pray "not my will be done but thine",
Fuse acceptance with great fear, scarcely up-
Held – never are you more son of man and son
of the Father. You drink the dreadful cup.
Your disciples slumber, every last one.
You quail, obey, doubt, suffer for our sake –
Refuse the drug: and you die wide awake!

3/30

I am that vagabond in exile, yet
Into my earth-mind, like the springtime snow-
Flake on the new bud, mysterious, wet,
(Thy truth like lace upon my need-to-know)
Falls gentle insight as I see thy word
In every exquisite and tiny bird
Or seed; as in the tragic and absurd.

3/31

It is so terrible to contemplate –
Thy passion, willingness, fear, doubt and death.
So, on thy cross we too take our last breath,
Become thy siblings in this awful fate.
I think there was more agony between
Thy dying question and the firstbirth keen
Into the paradise past mercy-gate.

APRIL.

1.

LORD, I do choose the higher than my will.
I would be handled by thy nursing arms
After thy will, not my infant alarms.
Hurt me thou wilt – but then more loving still,
If more can be and less, in love's perfect zone!
My fancy shrinks from least of all thy harms,
But do thy will with me – I am thine own.

2.

Some things wilt thou not one day turn to dreams?
Some dreams wilt thou not one day turn to fact?
The thing that painful, more than should be, seems,
Shall not thy sliding years with them retract –
Shall fair realities not counteract?
The thing that was well dreamed of bliss and joy –
Wilt thou not breathe thy life into the toy?

3.

I have had dreams of absolute delight,
Beyond all waking bliss – only of grass,
Flowers, wind, a peak, a limb of marble white;
They dwell with me like things half come to pass,
True prophecies: – when I with thee am right,
If I pray, waking, for such a joy of sight,
Thou with the gold, wilt not refuse the brass.

APRIL

4/1

Lord, I too choose thy will, not mine, and fear
Being too dull to discern thy leading:
Missing the garden, obsessed by weeding,
Getting distracted, bringing up the rear,
Salty as Lot's wife, guided by thy rod;
Make me good, grateful for stripes I'm needing.
Please be my parent and teacher and seer.

4/2

As memory of the past turns to a dream,
And evanescent prophesies come true,
May joys we forfeit here resplendent gleam
In realms above. When we, on earth and blue,
Through empty spoken consolations, new
And old, hear loved ones breathe beyond seeing –
Surely you will love us into being!

4/3

I am of silver, pewter, peasant tin.
My dreams reflect the threat of war's abyss.
Yet I who count the nut-hatch as my kin
Live in a dream come true, and if I miss
The shape of things to come, I praise your Name
With every breath as my dear brothers maim/
Kill Allah's loved children with Judas-kiss.

4.

I think I shall not ever pray for such;
Thy bliss will overflood my heart and brain,
And I want no unripe things back again.
Love ever fresher, lovelier than of old –
How should it want its more exchanged for much?
Love will not backward sigh, but forward strain,
On in the tale still telling, never told.

5.

What has been, shall not only be, but is.
The hues of dreamland, strange and sweet and tender
Are but hint-shadows of full many a splendour
Which the high Parent-love will yet unroll
Before his child's obedient, humble soul.
Ah, me, my God! in thee lies every bliss
Whose shadow men go hunting wearily amiss.

6.

Now, ere I sleep, I wonder what I shall dream.
Some sense of being, utter new, may come
Into my soul while I am blind and dumb –
With shapes and airs and scents which dark hours teem,
Of other sort than those that haunt the day,
Hinting at precious things, ages away
In the long tale of us God to himself doth say.

7.

Late, in a dream, an unknown lady I saw
Stand on a tomb; down she to me stepped thence.
"They tell me," quoth I, "thou art one of the dead!"
And scarce believed for gladness the yea she said;
A strange auroral bliss, an arctic awe,
A new, outworldish joy awoke intense,
To think I talked with one that verily was dead.

4/4

This man receives the body of thy host
Within the mystery of death, the deep;
Foregoes temptations of the new to keep
Planting the ripest truth-seed from thy core.
Not in the convert's field of many/more –
But in the love of tried and true, thy *most* –
Tells he (in silence) how to sing/adore.

4/5

Can past sins/present/future hopes be one?
Our shadow-actions and the great Beyond
Entwined, the mobius upon the wand,
Ourselves there crucified in abject hope –
The anguished sinner and the upheld pope;
Is *this* the promised day (thy word concise)
We are to be with thee in Paradise?

4/6

Dream as prayer! As on the waking tree
Of time (*present* between the *past* thief
And the one who *shall be* in paradise)
Our horizontal passion comes to be;
So in the night, breathing/breathed, the brief,
Vertical meditations fall and rise....
Mysterious parables, deep and wise.

4/7

Myself already dead, I hope to find
The grace to enter into my right mind;
In dreams the strength to turn the mystic key
That locks this earthly door, that I may see
The seventh heaven, and the living tree.
Just now, a white-tailed doe I often fed
Lies at pond edge; a hunter shot her dead.

8.

Thou dost demand our love, holy Lord Christ,
And batest nothing of thy modesty; –
Thou know'st no other way to bliss the highest
Than loving thee, the loving, perfectly.
Thou lovest perfectly – that is thy bliss:
We must love like thee, or our being miss –
So, to love perfectly, love perfect Love, love thee.

9.

Here is my heart, O Christ; thou know'st I love thee.
But wretched is the thing I call my love.
O Love divine, rise up in me and move me –
I follow surely when thou first dost move.
To love the perfect love, is primal, mere
Necessity; and he who holds life dear,
Must love thee every hope and heart above.

10.

Might I but scatter interfering things –
Questions and doubts, distrusts and anxious pride,
And in thy garment, as under gathering wings,
Nestle obedient to thy loving side,
Easy it were to love thee. But when thou
Send'st me to think and labour from thee wide,
Love falls to asking many a why and how.

11.

Easier it were, but poorer were the love.
Lord, I would have me love thee from the deeps –
Of troubled thought, of pain, of weariness.
Through seething wastes below, billows above,
My soul should rise in eager, hungering leaps;
Through thorny thicks, through sands unstable press –
Out of my dream to him who slumbers not nor sleeps.

4/8

I cannot help but love; didst thou demand?
I strive to love my neighbors – that is hard
As to accept myself without despair.
I love thee not by edict but like land
Or stars created by a genius bard.
I love thee, Lord of love, thou art my air –
But to love *perfectly*? How do I dare?

4/9

Here is my heart, but Lord, I have to card
Continually thistles from this wool.
Restraining *runneth-over* love is hard –
How not to worship man when joy is full?
How to hold close with open arms instead
Of longing to attract, possess and wed
The lightning of Europa's god-white bull?

4/10

Heal me ongoingly with spit and mud.
I wish to be thy footstool, covered by
Thy brooding hem which saves from loss of blood;
My thoughts and feelings flat beneath thy thigh
Like vows, safe from the fire and the flood.
Form thou my conscience; I am prostrate here
Within your peace, deaf to world chaos fear.

4/11

Having lost all, a loser, pinioned down
Like Gulliver, contained and immobile;
I send my little prayer for help to thee,
Doing my errands in this tiny town.
What I would further like to learn, to seal
Resolve, is how when most lost and cast-down
To give more thanks the more the pain I feel.

12.

I do not fear the greatness of thy command –
To keep heart-open-house to brother men;
But till in thy God's love perfect I stand,
My door not wide enough will open. Then
Each man will be love-awful in my sight;
And, open to the eternal morning's might,
Each human face will shine my window for thy light.

13.

Make me all patience and all diligence;
Patience, that thou mayst have thy time with me;
Diligence, that I waste not thy expense
In sending out to bring me home to thee.
What though thy work in me transcends my sense –
Too fine, too high, for me to understand –
I hope entirely. On, Lord, with thy labour grand.

14.

Lest I be humbled at the last, and told
That my great labour was but for my peace;
That not for love or truth had I been bold,
But merely for a prisoned heart's release;
Careful, I humble me now before thy feet:
Whate'er I be, I cry, and will not cease –
Let me not perish, though favour be not meet.

15.

For, what I seek thou knowest I must find,
Or miserably die for lack of love.
I justify thee: what is in thy mind,
If it be shame to me, all shame above.
Thou know'st I choose it – know'st I would not shove
The hand away that stripped me for the rod –
If so it pleased my Life, my love-made-angry God.

4/12

I cannot see my neighbor for my pain.
I try to take right actions, while inside,
The sniper cuts through my defeated brain
To tell me I can neither love nor hide.
To feed the beggar, knowing myself such,
I must restrain my own voracious need
From tainting kindness with despair and greed.

4/13

Yes, lead me on, Lord, despite all my flaws,
Through this new day of my new-blesséd life.
Help me to feel again thy solemn laws
As birdcalls sing sublime upon thy fife.
Lead me 'till dead ends turn me to thy way –
Straighter and narrower, in stillness clear,
By dreams of night and light of springtime day.

4/14

I am thy penitent and scarce stand up,
Not being strong enough to keep, sustain
The sense of thy forgiveness in my cup
(Of Abel's clay, fired in the kiln of Cain).
When Maundy Thursday and Passover meet,
May I invite Barabbas in to eat,
And kneel to wash Elijah's tired feet?

4/15

"Father knows best"! I, fatherless, now know...
If you would love me enough to forbid,
I can accept that life may be a blow
Correcting willful wrongdoings I did.
Shall I so shamed and bleeding run to you
With every little scrape and big heartbreak,
And give up earthly seeking for your sake?

16.

I see a door, a multitude near by,
In creed and quarrel, sure disciples all!
Gladly they would, they say, enter the hall,
But cannot, the stone threshold is so high.
From unseen hand, full many a feeding crumb,
Slow dropping o'er the threshold high doth come:
They gather and eat, with much disputing hum.

17.

Still and anon, a loud clear voice doth call –
"Make your feet clean, and enter so the hall."
They hear, they stoop, they gather each a crumb.
Oh the deaf people! would they were also dumb!
Hear how they talk, and lack of Christ deplore,
Stamping with muddy feet about the door,
And will not wipe them clean to walk upon his floor!

18.

But see, one comes; he listens to the voice;
Careful he wipes his weary dusty feet!
The voice hath spoken – to him is left no choice;
He hurries to obey – that only is meet.
Low sinks the threshold, levelled with the ground;
The man leaps in – to liberty he's bound.
The rest go talking, walking, picking round.

19.

If I, thus writing, rebuke my neighbour dull,
And talk, and write, and enter not the door,
Than all the rest I wrong Christ tenfold more,
Making his gift of vision void and null.
Help me this day to be thy humble sheep,
Eating thy grass, and following, thou before;
From wolfish lies my life, O Shepherd, keep.

4/16

Talmudic disputations fuel our zest,
Exactitude is sought (manna of stone)
And mystery is hard to bear alone;
The letting go of *good* that rivals *best*.
So may a famished outcast sparrow bird –
While following a crust of rote absurd –
Find just the crumb that leads to life and word!

4/17

Bruised Moses leads us through the sea of reeds!
Consecrated firstborns, unleavened, bow
As everywhere on earth the pierced one bleeds.
We drink this holy wine in Pesach cup
And Pascha chalice, as we offer up
With washed hands/Maundy Thursday's narded feet –
Love crucified upon the Mercy seat.

4/18

The way into "the next room of the dream"?
Obedience. Theologians, well-shod,
Are loathe to show bare feet to man or God.
Their calloused, crooked toes must surely seem
Like animals'; they'd have to lose all pride,
(The washer and the washed, baptismal tide)
To step out of the dust – become the bride.

4/19

If I (who do not yet have sense to know
Aught but "the mercy of the fallen") do
The best I can, discerning old and new
Voice – lamb's blood on both lintel and cross; who
Is this sly accuser within saying
I've not done enough, my work's useless woe,
And takes time away from humble praying?

20.

God, help me, dull of heart, to trust in thee.
Thou art the father of me – not any mood
Can part me from the One, the verily Good.
When fog and failure o'er my being brood.
When life looks but a glimmering marshy clod,
No fire out flashing from the living God –
Then, then, to rest in faith were worthy victory!

21.

To trust is gain and growth, not mere sown seed!
Faith heaves the world round to the heavenly dawn,
In whose great light the soul doth spell and read
Itself high-born, its being derived and drawn
From the eternal self-existent fire;
Then, mazed with joy of its own heavenly breed,
Exultant-humble falls before its awful sire.

22.

Art thou not, Jesus, busy like to us?
Thee shall I image as one sitting still,
Ordering all things in thy potent will,
Silent, and thinking ever to thy father,
Whose thought through thee flows multitudinous?
Or shall I think of thee as journeying, rather,
Ceaseless through space, because thou everything dost fill?

23.

That all things thou dost fill, I well may think –
Thy power doth reach me in so many ways.
Thou who in one the universe dost bind,
Passest through all the channels of my mind;
The sun of thought, across the farthest brink
Of consciousness thou sendest me thy rays;
Nor drawest them in when lost in sleep I sink.

4/20

I rest in faith on this bright day. The green
New leaves emerge from shrouds of gentle rose,
The consecrated breads of Easter doughs
Break; world egg waits to hatch thy purpose, knows
Thy inexplicable comforter, Love,
Whispering softly from within+above,
I am with thee, infinite, sweet, unseen.

4/21

Today the holy fire within thy sun,
Tonight the blue-lit meteor shower;
Way, truth and life, you are the One
Of galaxies and this small white flower.
Breathe into me, Lord, such wonder, child's trust,
That I may by the moment and hour
Be born with tears as living clay from dust!

4/22

I smell good earth beside the grave of death;
Sigh thanks that for late-bloomers you will wait.
I think of you as brother and as breath,
As pearl beside whom everyone is naught –
Light as the breeze and precious as a mate
With whom one may dare anything; the thought
That stops me spinning like a circus plate.

4/23

We marinated beings live in hope
That even though we float askew or dim,
You have us by a sturdy, holy rope;
Can reel us home on tendril of a hymn.
Illuminated manuscripts we are...
Each day a page, each night a little star –
Remember us, Lord, be we near or far!

24.

So common are thy paths, thy coming seems
Only another phase oft of my *me*;
But nearer is my *I*, O Lord, to thee,
Than is my *I* to what itself it deems;
How better then couldst thou, O Master, come,
Than from thy home across into my home,
Straight o'er the marches that I cannot see!

25.

Marches? – 'Twixt thee and me there's no division,
Except the meeting of thy will and mine,
The loves that love, the wills that will the same.
Where thine meets mine is my life's true condition;
Yea, only there it burns with any flame.
Thy will but holds me to my life's fruition.
O God, I would – I have no mine that is not thine.

26.

I look for thee, and do not see thee come. –
If I could see thee, 'twere a commoner thing,
And shallower comfort would thy coming bring.
Earth, sea, and air lie round me moveless dumb,
Never a tremble, an expectant hum,
To tell the Lord of Hearts is drawing near:
Lo! in the looking eyes, the looked for Lord is here.

27.

I take a comfort from my very badness:
It is for lack of thee that I am bad.
How close, how infinitely closer yet
Must I come to thee, ere I can pay one debt
Which mere humanity has on me set!
"How close to thee!" – no wonder, soul, thou art glad!
Oneness with him is the eternal gladness.

4/24

Expect the unexpected, it is said;
Especially surprise which comes as grace!
Last night when my *i* went in grief to bed,
She little dreamed the joy you'd put in place.
Darkest before dawn; only sleepers wake!
Can it be true I am not a mistake,
And have now dancing orders for your sake?

4/25

Take wheat and weeds of me, Lord, woven sweet,
And may I always choose the better part;
To keep my famished listening at thy feet,
Aspiring to be burnished in thy heart.
Wed deep in me willingness and thy will
(With every word of electronic quill)
May I, thy bride, believe you love me still.

4/26

Though blind, we kingdoms/vast cathedrals see!
Music! In seeking, finding comes to be;
Beyond eyesight-proof lives reality,
Lost & Found linked by graceful ampersand,
So like the treble clef in which the hand
& line set cursive spirals through rain-sun
That twine to heaven – call/response are one.

4/27

Lord, why does love hurt so much? Tell me, please.
Over and over again, on my knees,
I ask, "Why are my loves so far from sane,
Hungering, jealous, raging, needy, vain?"
Teach me within the heart of your embrace,
To enter longing at a different place,
And become one with gratitude and grace.

28.

What can there be so close as *making* and *made*?
Nought twinned can be so near; thou art more nigh
To me, my God, than is this thinking *I*
To that I mean when *I* by me is said;
Thou art more near me, than is my ready will
Near to my love, though both one place do fill; –
Yet, till we are one, – Ah me! the long *until!*

29.

Then shall my heart behold thee everywhere.
The vision rises of a speechless thing,
A perfectness of bliss beyond compare!
A time when I nor breathe nor think nor move,
But I do breathe and think and feel thy love,
The soul of all the songs the saints do sing! –
And life dies out in bliss, to come again in prayer.

30.

In the great glow of that great love, this death
Would melt away like a fantastic cloud;
I should no more shrink from it than from the breath
That makes in the frosty air a nimbus-shroud;
Thou, Love, hast conquered death, and I aloud
Should triumph over him, with thy saintly crowd,
That where the Lamb goes ever followeth.

4/28

There is a space between me and my name,
(Although I see thy stamp upon the face
And spirit of the joyous child i was) –
Between thought/word and between that and this.
O, set thy seal upon this brow of shame.
There, in meditation's orange-dawn bliss,
Beats the one blood song of our august race.

4/29

Just now the green is edging from the bud.
Bloom itself has begun. Out of spit-mud,
The kind that makes us blind ones grow and see
Into the very heart of mystery
Enkindled in love's eyes; so, day and night,
Men may root and family trees take flight –
Watered by rain and fragrant tides of light!

4/30

As one who could not follow women through
The nimbus labor 'round their giving birth,
So am no mother; as a dumbstruck Jew
And blacksheep, come so late to thee on earth –
A fearful, city-slaughtered, blemished lamb –
Help me through death/birth-3, from naysay's clan,
To dare to call upon the son of man!

MAY.

1.

WHAT though my words glance sideways from the thing
Which I would utter in thine ear, my sire!
Truth in the inward parts thou dost desire –
Wise hunger, not a fitness fine of speech:
The little child that clamouring fails to reach
With upstretched hand the fringe of her attire,
Yet meets the mother's hand down hurrying.

2.

Even when their foolish words they turned on him,
He did not his disciples send away;
He knew their hearts were foolish, eyes were dim,
And therefore by his side needs must they stay.
Thou will not, Lord, send me away from thee.
When I am foolish, make thy cock crow grim;
If that is not enough, turn, Lord, and look on me.

3.

Another day of gloom and slanting rain!
Of closed skies, cold winds, and blight and bane!
Such not the weather, Lord, which thou art fain
To give thy chosen, sweet to heart and brain! –
Until we mourn, thou keep'st the merry tune;
Thy hand unloved its pleasure must restrain,
Nor spoil both gift and child by lavishing too soon.

MAY

5/1

Wise hunger, just to know and do thy will –
To seek thee, seeking find thee in the heart
Which beats in ceaseless prayer; breath as art –
Who sings psalms prays twice, keening we shed strife,
To mourn our dead and celebrate the life
Of spirit housed in fragile, wondrous clay
That cloaks like dusk, then dawns and breaks like day!

5/2

Look on me, Lord, newborn and feeling small,
Dull, old, a glutton, foolish, lacking love,
Forgiven much but seeing only flaws.
Did thy disciples know themselves at all?
Were they eclipsed by thy light from above,
As they walked with you, plowing up old laws,
Saved from husk-dogma by thy holy cause?

5/3

A glorious day of hard rain falling –
Under the downpour, my heart is calling:
Thanks, Lord, for minting me, new, evergreen,
Filling my soul with thanksgiving this keen;
Raining such blessings as bring me to tears,
Washing away my life's anguish and fears,
Bringing redemption, sweet, peaceful and clean!

4.

But all things shall be ours! Up, heart, and sing.
All things were made for us – we are God's heirs –
Moon, sun, and wildest comets that do trail
A crowd of small worlds for a swiftness-tail!
Up from Thy depths in me, my child-heart bring –
The child alone inherits anything:
God's little children-gods – all things are theirs!

5.

Thy great deliverance is a greater thing
Than purest imagination can foregrasp;
A thing beyond all conscious hungering,
Beyond all hope that makes the poet sing.
It takes the clinging world, undoes its clasp,
Floats it afar upon a mighty sea,
And leaves us quiet with love and liberty and thee.

6.

Through all the fog, through all earth's wintery sighs,
I scent Thy spring, I feel the eternal air,
Warm, soft, and dewy, filled with flowery eyes,
And gentle, murmuring motions everywhere –
Of life in heart, and tree, and brook, and moss;
Thy breath wakes beauty, love, and bliss, and prayer,
And strength to hang with nails upon thy cross.

7.

If thou hadst closed my life in seed and husk,
And cast me into soft, warm, damp, dark mould,
All unaware of light come through the dusk,
I yet should feel the split of each shelly fold,
Should feel the growing of my prisoned heart,
And dully dream of being slow unrolled,
And in some other vagueness taking part.

5/4

With laser lovelight, shell me like a pea!
Let me see through my own unknown deceit,
Until I come as I am to your feet,
To marvel that as you parted the sea,
And walked on windy water, I may stand,
Ever so far away from this dry land,
Out of the old pod, thankful, green, and free.

5/5

Unclasp all concepts; float away this dream,
Shed ideas and constructions like old skin –
Step out into bright newness every day
And trust that God in time will show thy way.
So wonderful that we may be his kin;
So marvelous to be forgiven sin –
Such awesome blooming in this month of May!

5/6

Each season sings out its most profound key;
Autumnal sacrifices herald spring –
A summer lives within stark winter's dream.
An appleseed may truly come to bring
Through dread ice storms a sturdy living tree.
The sigh that leaves the soul in grief and death,
May lift a dandelion by its breath.

5/7

Spiraling up from ferny, mossy vales,
In spiritual photosynthesis,
We fronds unfurl despite our mouldy shrouds,
Into thy realm of simple, fragrant bliss,
Green as this hill of grass and bright grey clouds,
New leaves and lives come blooming through travails –
Watered by gardener pierced by spear and nails!

8.

And little as the world I should foreknow
Up into which I was about to rise –
Its rains, its radiance, airs, and warmth, and skies,
How it would greet me, how its wind would blow –
As little, it may be, I do know the good
Which I for years half darkling have pursued –
The second birth for which my nature cries.

9.

The life that knows not, patient waits, nor longs: –
I know, and would be patient, yet would long.
I can be patient for all coming songs,
But let me sing my one monotonous song.
To me the time is slow my mould among;
To quicker life I fain would spur and start
The aching growth at my dull-swelling heart.

10.

Christ is the pledge that I shall one day see;
That one day, still with him, I shall awake,
And know my God, at one with him and free.
O lordly essence, come to life in me;
The will-throb let me feel that doth me make;
Now have I many a mighty hope in thee,
Then shall I rest although the universe should quake.

11.

Haste to me, Lord, when this fool-heart of mine
Begins to gnaw itself with selfish craving;
Or, like a foul thing scarcely worth the saving,
Swoln up with wrath, desireth vengeance fine.
Haste, Lord, to help, when reason favours wrong;
Haste when thy soul, the high-born thing divine,
Is torn by passion's raving, maniac throng.

5/8

And, having glimpsed – in ecstasy or tear,
In bird or flower, child's face, human hand –
The sure existence of a higher realm
Beyond imagining, why do we fear?
Our longing leads us toward an unknown land.
Here in root-intuition of the elm,
We *deepen wonder*, know, love, bloom and hear!

5/9

I know not: still, I wait, and my heart longs
For the unknown as for the *Song of Songs*.
My certainty about this afterlife
Rests with my imperfectibility.
I walk the high road of your *Book of Strife*,
Slowly, with each day dawning, as I see
That in God's time he'll change/illumine me.

5/10

Blessed are they who believe without proof.
You are my brother. That is all I know.
If I should doubt, lower me through thy roof!
Until I knew thee, all my life was woe.
Be with me, Jesus, when God seems aloof.
Galaxies quake now, somehow on we go –
Thy quiet word heard though cyclone winds blow.

5/11

See us beyond these rapids, darling Lord.
In thy serene canoe of birchbark white,
Throw my resentments, furies, overboard,
That I may drift in thee, both deep and light;
Back to the drummer-heart that beats and prays,
Reborn in solace of thy springtime days,
Singing to pintail ducks as they take flight.

12.

Fair freshness of the God-breathed spirit air,
Pass through my soul, and make it strong to love;
Wither with gracious cold what demons dare
Shoot from my hell into my world above;
Let them drop down, like leaves the sun doth sear,
And flutter far into the inane and bare,
Leaving my middle-earth calm, wise, and clear.

13.

Even thou canst give me neither thought nor thing,
Were it the priceless pearl hid in the land,
Which, if I fix thereon a greedy gaze,
Becomes not poison that doth burn and cling;
Their own bad look my foolish eyes doth daze,
They see the gift, see not the giving hand –
From the living root the apple dead I wring.

14.

This versing, even the reading of the tale
That brings my heart its joy unspeakable,
Sometimes will softly, unsuspectedly hale
That heart from thee, and all its pulses quell.
Discovery's pride, joy's bliss, take aback my sail,
And sweep me from thy presence and my grace,
Because my eyes dropped from the master's face.

15.

Afresh I seek thee. Lead me – once more I pray –
Even should it be against my will, thy way.
Let me not feel thee foreign any hour,
Or shrink from thee as an estranged power.
Through doubt, through faith, through bliss, through stark dismay,
Through sunshine, wind, or snow, or fog, or shower,
Draw me to thee who art my only day.

5/12

Listening to talk radio's loud zest –
A caller speaks well of *Lord of the Rings*,
Next a lapsed Catholic rails against Mother
Teresa – I saw my faults as the best
Ballast – weights laid upon my training wings.
I no longer fear sister or brother,
And dare to be my flaw-ful self in quest.

5/13

I must keep my eyes ongoingly peeled,
Like onion-skins that make me cry (to see
The more I see the more I longing sigh)
Or keep nun's custody and thus be healed
Of all I love and crave at first sight; die
Wanting too much to be apple of thy
Eye – to carve my heart within thy bark, Tree!

5/14

I wish to spiral, growing within thee,
For when I worship cross or house of wood,
Or think my white-page poems any good,
Pride/folly/avarice my masters be,
And I sink quicksand in the Land of Me.
Do keep me floating safe within thy barque,
And with thy Spirit raise the rainbow ark.

5/15

Leave me not here (discouragement abyss)
Nor here (paralysis analysis)
Nor here (seeking a clear and certain sign)
Nor chipping diamonds from the daily mine.
The more I rise, the more I am assailed.
My fears have half-convinced me I have failed –
'Round Eden's tree, I hear the serpent hiss.

16.

I would go near thee – but I cannot press
Into thy presence – it helps not to presume.
Thy doors are deeds; the handles are their doing.
He whose day-life is obedient righteousness,
Who, after failure, or a poor success,
Rises up, stronger effort yet renewing –
He finds thee, Lord, at length, in his own common room.

17.

Lord, thou hast carried me through this evening's duty;
I am released, weary, and well content.
O soul, put on the evening dress of beauty,
Thy sunset-flush, of gold and purple blent! –
Alas, the moment I turn to my heart,
Feeling runs out of doors, or stands apart!
But such as I am, Lord, take me as thou art.

18.

The word he then did speak, fits now as then,
For the same kind of men doth mock at it.
God-fools, God-drunkards these do call the men
Who think the poverty of their all not fit,
Borne humbly by their art, their voice, their pen,
Save for its allness, at thy feet to fling,
For whom all is unfit that is not everything.

19.

O Christ, my life, possess me utterly.
Take me and make a little Christ of me.
If I am anything but thy father's son,
'Tis something not yet from the darkness won.
Oh, give me light to live with open eyes.
Oh, give me life to hope above all skies.
Give me thy spirit to haunt the Father with my cries.

5/16

Cows on the hill, beyond the SUV's –
I pause to say your prayer on my knees –
Next save the mayfly, taking her outside
In a tin cup (pink lemonade scent). Guide
Her brief life, Lord! A blessed, fragile calm;
Old dog and kitten sleep. Gilead's balm
Annoints me – you are here and you abide.

5/17

Lord, thou hast led me through this Sabbath day;
I watch thy greenstick dowser wand in play –
It leads to water – is this meant for me?
Show me thy will within this springtime tree.
Scattering anecdotes like birdseed, I
Thank thee for every moment passing by,
And for the souls who help me live and die.

5/18

All of me: breath, blood, dreams, hope, art, love, faith –
As the potter's fingerprints mark this clay –
I give thee, Father. Although a dim wraith,
An aging bone-chalice, I learn to play,
Blindfolded, spiraling, returning praise,
Glad to be thine in this nature/these days,
Use, fill, and seal me, Word, in all thy ways.

5/19

O Christ, my life, meet me at fountain-well.
Give me (Samarian and Magdalene),
Communion (sparrow on the rainy stone),
Assurance that as I am, I am seen;
That as you liberated me from hell
And showed me sure that I am not alone –
I may now be adopted by thy Queen!

20.

'Tis hard for man to rouse his spirit up –
It is the human creative agony,
Though but to hold the heart an empty cup,
Or tighten on the team the rigid rein.
Many will rather lie among the slain
Than creep through narrow ways the light to gain –
Than wake the will, and be born bitterly.

21.

But he who would be born again indeed,
Must wake his soul unnumbered times a day,
And urge himself to life with holy greed;
Now ope his bosom to the Wind's free play;
And now, with patience forceful, hard, lie still,
Submiss and ready to the making will,
Athirst and empty, for God's breath to fill.

22.

All times are thine whose will is our remede.
Man turns to thee, thou hast not turned away;
The look he casts, thy labour that did breed –
It is thy work, thy business all the day:
That look, not foregone fitness, thou dost heed.
For duty absolute how be fitter than now?
Or learn by shunning? – Lord, I come; help thou.

23.

Ever above my coldness and my doubt
Rises up something, reaching forth a hand:
This thing I know, but cannot understand.
Is it the God in me that rises out
Beyond my self, trailing it up with him,
Towards the spirit-home, the freedom-land,
Beyond my conscious ken, my near horizon's brim?

5/20

Be born bitterly through platitudes by
Those innocents whose faith is sweet and fine;
Be born bitterly through the darkened mine,
Be new-created, so create new line –
Be born bitterly from will-cocoon debts –
Sad, wet-winged, fragile in the Land of Nets,
An irridescence, soon to dry and fly!

5/21

Yesterday's manna will not do today;
We wake newborn, begin to breathe and pray,
Else rage or dream the gift of hours away,
Buy groceries, tremble as the war draws near.
Poor, chaste, obedient, we exhaust fear,
In anguish hope, and bless the wind that blows,
Knowing you know us in our sparrow clothes.

5/22

Just as we are, souls who turn free to thee,
We shall be woven in thy warp and weft;
Wholecloth and patchworks too in thy will, wise
Weaver, horizontal/vertical be
Cross-prayers, shuttling, seeking right to left,
Heaven-earth sailcloths, the fabric of sighs,
Comforters – armor in eiderdown guise!

5/23

Longing itself, the heartfelt, wordless cry
As, dying, pruned and growing, we persist;
Breaking earth's atmosphere as seed breaks sod
To live in the reality of God;
Jack's beanstalk, up and out, the cross in sky
We climb to justice and to mercy high,
Striving by rod/staff solace, *to exist.*

24.

O God of man, my heart would worship all
My fellow men, the flashes from thy fire;
Them in good sooth my lofty kindred call,
Born of the same one heart, the perfect sire;
Love of my kind alone can set me free;
Help me to welcome all that come to me,
Not close my doors and dream solitude liberty!

25.

A loving word may set some door ajar
Where seemed no door, and that may enter in
Which lay at the heart of that same loving word.
In my still chamber dwell thou always, Lord;
Thy presence there will carriage true afford;
True words will flow, pure of design to win;
And to my men my door shall have no bar.

26.

My prayers, my God, flow from what I am not;
I think thy answers make me what I am.
Like weary waves thought follows upon thought,
But the still depth beneath is all thine own,
And there thou mov'st in paths to us unknown.
Out of strange strife thy peace is strangely wrought;
If the lion in us pray – thou answerest the lamb.

27.

So bound in selfishness am I, so chained,
I know it must be glorious to be free
But know not what, full-fraught, the word doth mean.
By loss on loss I have severely gained
Wisdom enough my slavery to see;
But liberty, pure, absolute, serene,
No freëst-visioned slave has ever seen.

5/24

Years in subways, city streets, guardedly
Moving through my life, gathering no moss;
Those of my kind are seared by tragic loss.
Beggars and madfolk mostly come to me
For I myself am crazed, and wounded be.
My solitude is gratitude, release,
Dream, consolation, torment, hope and peace.

5/25

I scarcely can receive, can only give;
Doubt on my loving words one long could live.
My dad was absence, unknown, old snapshot,
Cad, doctor, boyish master of heart-heist.
I had to find Our Father via Christ.
When jilted mother's love became too hot,
I was her icon: please, adore me not!

5/26

This black sheep quakes – I see my elders shorn!
In swift time-currents I am swept away –
Within: *be still*, and in the depths: *I am*...
Am washed up past the waterfall, reborn.
My breath restored, catch-as-catch-can, I pray
To lie down with the lion, night and day,
And be in time God's own unblemished lamb.

5/27

Free me to be, not mourn what might-have-been.
There is no I here, it is false, and yet
I am trapped in a gauze of me's and my's
As though, to be true, "I" had to bag sin
Swiftly, with a hand-made butterfly net,
Then walk the world, bottled, in human guise,
With air-holes pierced to let the Spirit in...

28.

For, that great freedom how should such as I
Be able to imagine in such a self?
Less hopeless far the miser man might try
To image the delight of friend-shared pelf.
Freedom is to be like thee, face and heart;
To know it, Lord, I must be as thou art,
I cannot breed the imagination high.

29.

Yet hints come to me from the realm unknown;
Airs drift across the twilight border land,
Odoured with life; and as from some far strand
Sea-murmured, whispers to my heart are blown
That fill me with a joy I cannot speak,
Yea, from whose shadow words drop faint and weak:
Thee, God, I shadow in that region grand.

30.

O Christ, who didst appear in Judah land,
Thence by the cross go back to God's right hand,
Plain history, and things our sense beyond,
In thee together come and correspond:
How rulest thou from the undiscovered bourne
The world-wise world that laughs thee still to scorn?
Please, Lord, let thy disciple understand.

31.

'Tis heart on heart thou rulest. Thou art the same
At God's right hand as here exposed to shame,
And therefore workest now as thou didst then –
Feeding the faint divine in humble men.
Through all thy realms from thee goes out heart-power,
Working the holy, satisfying hour,
When all shall love, and all be loved again.

5/28

I cannot feel that I am at all free,
And to be like thee is a task so great,
Despair might fill my cell-without-a-key.
You have no home and wander, serving God...
Are feared, mocked, killed/forgiving. Liberty!
'Tis hard enough to break this crust of sod,
As dream to be a green pea in thy pod.

5/29

The wonderful perfection of earth-loam,
The happy motor of my little cat,
Remind me that although I have no home
(Save for this refuge where I hang my hat)
The spiral prayers, like the phoebe's art,
Return this knowledge: we are truly part
And parcel of the Master's mystic heart.

5/30

From crucified and contrite broken hearts,
Though ancient chants sent forth heard no reply –
There is a mercy tide, and this sea parts
To let the frightened gratitudes go by;
Spiraling divine Soul, essential, free –
Transforming root and fruit of this great tree –
Taste the Fountain of Immortality!

5/31

Can it be that though here, failing in love,
Something of us is shining from above?
That as we lose in ways that make us wise,
New beings win in realms beyond the skies?
That as we spiral down in shame and up
In aspiration you will fill the cup
Of our hearts full enough to quench our cries?

JUNE.

1.

FROM thine, as then, the healing virtue goes
Into our hearts – that is the Father's plan.
From heart to heart it sinks, it steals, it flows,
From these that know thee still infecting those.
Here is my heart – from thine, Lord, fill it up,
That I may offer it as the holy cup
Of thy communion to my every man.

2.

When thou dost send out whirlwinds on thy seas,
Alternatest thy lightning with its roar,
Thy night with morning, and thy clouds with stars
Or, mightier force unseen in midst of these,
Orderest the life in every airy pore;
Guidest men's efforts, rul'st mishaps and jars, –
'Tis only for their hearts, and nothing more.

3.

This, this alone thy father careth for –
That men should live hearted throughout with thee –
Because the simple, only life thou art,
Of the very truth of living, the pure heart.
For this, deep waters whelm the fruitful lea,
Wars ravage, famine wastes, plague withers, nor
Shall cease till men have chosen the better part.

JUNE

6/1

May we be harvest, Lord – threshed from the dead! –
Empty and beaten, by still waters led;
Called into union, harrowed so by you,
We will to die, to hear, to dare, to do.
At holy banquet, far beyond all doubt,
Make us this day into thy blood and bread,
Fit to be broken, and to be poured out.

6/2

Remind me, Lord, by rippling, chartreuse light
Upon the underside of new green leaves –
Your summer is a harvest grace so bright,
Wonder and thanks entwine beneath the eaves,
Infinity and stillness filled with thee,
Beyond/within all I can feel or see....
May thankful tears bless what this fool believes!

6/3

Pure heart, your reasoning is simple, sweet;
To equate Martha's whirlwind with the flood,
See devastations as pulling our coat,
Until we love thy lamb and shoo scapegoat –
As acts of God, disasters, seas of blood
Meant to get our attention until, beat,
We sit in awe with Mary at thy feet.

4.

But, like a virtuous medicine, self-diffused
Through all men's hearts thy love shall sink and float;
Till every feeling false, and thought unwise,
Selfish, and seeking, shall, sternly disused,
Wither, and die, and shrivel up to nought;
And Christ, whom they did hang 'twixt earth and skies,
Up in the inner world of men arise.

5.

Make me a fellow worker with thee, Christ;
Nought else befits a God-born energy;
Of all that's lovely, only lives the highest,
Lifing the rest that it shall never die.
Up I would be to help thee – for thou liest
Not, linen-swathed in Joseph's garden-tomb,
But walkest crowned, creation's heart and bloom.

6.

My God, when I would lift my heart to thee,
Imagination instantly doth set
A cloudy something, thin, and vast, and vague,
To stand for him who is the fact of me;
Then up the Will, and doth her weakness plague
To pay the heart her duty and her debt,
Showing the face that hearkeneth to the plea.

7.

And hence it comes that thou at times dost seem
To fade into an image of my mind;
I, dreamer, cover, hide thee up with dream, –
Thee, primal, individual entity! –
No likeness will I seek to frame or find,
But cry to that which thou dost choose to be,
To that which is my sight, therefore I cannot see.

6/4

As we take up dry bones each day and walk
Into the day, both dying and renewed;
Thy holy blood dissolves the devil's caulk
And spirit floods our hearts with manna food.
May vestigial (snakeskin) sins abate,
And may we hang and rise, trees walking, great
In hope between thy garden and thy gate.

6/5

In foreign wars, potential husbands die –
"The flowers gone" infuse our hearts with peace.
May your true love in me find right release.
"Everything rising must converge" so high,
Each living soul is dearly blessed thereby.
Make me of use: our songs are here to sow;
Who reaps the harvest? That we need not know.

6/6

I have no image; only words that fail,
And flotsom time, and busy errand-haste.
The rain shrouds my intentions in its veil,
With disillusionments my dreams are laced.
I close my eyes and like a weary child
Seek infinite dimensions – there I know
My prayers rise to thee through moody woe.

6/7

I do not worship images of thee,
(Though I can feel the love in icon-paint)
Or understand the holy trinity,
(Or know what constitutes a living saint).
I stand with other children, fool and sage,
Astonished by the nature of this age,
And pray to keep believing, strong or faint.

8.

No likeness? Lo, the Christ! Oh, large Enough!
I see, yet fathom not the face he wore.
He is – and out of him there is no stuff
To make a man. Let fail me every spark
Of blissful vision on my pathway rough,
I have seen much, and trust the perfect more,
While to his feet my faith crosses the wayless dark.

9.

Faith is the human shadow of thy might.
Thou art the one self-perfect life, and we
Who trust thy life, therein join on to thee,
Taking our part in self-creating light.
To trust is to step forward out of the night –
To be – to share in the outgoing Will
That lives and is, because outgoing still.

10.

I am lost before thee, Father! yet I will
Claim of thee my birthright ineffable.
Thou lay'st it on me, son, to claim thee, sire;
To that which thou hast made me, I aspire;
To thee, the sun, upflames thy kindled fire.
No man presumes in that to which he was born;
Less than the gift to claim, would be the giver to scorn.

11.

Henceforth all things thy dealings are with me
For out of thee is nothing, or can be,
And all things are to draw us home to thee.
What matter that the knowers scoffing say,
"This is old folly, plain to the new day"? –
If thou be such as thou, and they as they,
Unto thy *Let there be*, they still must answer *Nay*.

6/8

One Word is worth a thousand pictured Christs;
None can contain or fix him finitely,
But cloak our seeking in arts' many veils,
Or channel, like a chanted rosary,
To stop imagination's many heists,
To see us through the miracles, the nails,
Into the incarnation's holy *We.*

6/9

Doubt is the shadow cast by faithful light –
Lengthening behind us, we step out in air.
Yes, amen, say we softly, as did she
Through whom our own redemption came to be.
God-bearing children, past the dragon-lair,
Leaving Lot's wife our salty tears, yes, bright
As small rising hope stars in this dark night.

6/10

Because my earthly father went away,
I cannot "claim", though I am truly yours;
And feel the living yearning every day
Deeper – I row with dowser rod/staff oars.
Shocked by my mother's age, fragility –
I am her daughter-god: she worships me.
Help me to bear these gifts, reborn and free!

6/11

What is thy will for me? O, Father, bless.
This *Let there be* – is it my own or thine?
When stand I forth against all *Nays* with *Yes*?
When say I *Nay* to things appearing fine?
Hair-splitting doubts assail me. Let me know
Even in small ways how I am to go
Looking for Eeyore's house, in rain and snow.

12.

They will not, therefore cannot, do not know him.
Nothing they could know, could be God. In sooth,
Unto the true alone exists the truth.
They say well, saying Nature doth not show him:
Truly she shows not what she cannot show;
And they deny the thing they cannot know.
Who sees a glory, towards it will go.

13.

Faster no step moves God because the fool
Shouts to the universe God there is none;
The blindest man will not preach out the sun,
Though on his darkness he should found a school.
It may be, when he finds he is not dead,
Though world and body, sight and sound are fled,
Some eyes may open in his foolish head.

14.

When I am very weary with hard thought,
And yet the question burns and is not quenched,
My heart grows cool when to remembrance wrought
That thou who know'st the light-born answer sought
Know'st too the dark where the doubt lies entrenched –
Know'st with what seemings I am sore perplexed,
And that with thee I wait, nor needs my soul be vexed.

15.

Who sets himself not sternly to be good,
Is but a fool, who judgment of true things
Has none, however oft the claim renewed.
And he who thinks, in his great plenitude,
To right himself, and set his spirit free,
Without the might of higher communings,
Is foolish also – save he willed himself to be.

6/12

The Second Coming heads the morning news;
Crusaders spin the gospel sacrifice,
Preaching for-profit wars. The youngbloods die;
None dare say treason. Real smart-bombs/cool blues
Play musak in tomb-malls where shoppers buy
Bright neon end-time whatnots. We throw rice
At the shotgun wedding of fear and vice.

6/13

Afraid to take action, undermined by
Whispers of warning and sly alibi,
I hesitate, am lost, divided, freeze.
This is death too, a swarm of thoughts, a hive
Of stinging questions eating me alive!
Dear Father, clarify my pathway, please,
And anchor me in peace upon my knees.

6/14

Through waiting and choice-weighing in thy calm...
Chapel of the tin roof in the hard rain,
The cross+mark in the center of the palm,
The solace of Gilead's ancient balm...
As courage coalesces out of pain,
And constancy of change illumines time –
Be thou the spirit-root of life and rhyme.

6/15

Here in the church of George, our brother, friend –
The truths are hard, the brogue is lilting sweet.
Those in front pews who pray "world without end",
Souls in the back with crumbs of word to eat,
Borderline fringe-folk – all give thanks today.
Our living Father, Lord of tenderest bliss...
Pray for us fatherless on days like this.

16.

How many helps thou giv'st to those would learn!
To some sore pain, to others a sinking heart;
To some a weariness worse than any smart;
To some a haunting, fearing, blind concern;
Madness to some; to some the shaking dart
Of hideous death still following as they turn;
To some a hunger that will not depart.

17.

To some thou giv'st a deep unrest – a scorn
Of all they are or see upon the earth;
A gaze, at dusky night and clearing morn,
As on a land of emptiness and dearth;
To some a bitter sorrow; to some the sting
Of love misprized – of sick abandoning;
To some a frozen heart, oh, worse than anything!

18.

To some a mocking demon, that doth set
The poor foiled will to scoff at the ideal,
But loathsome makes to them their life of jar.
The messengers of Satan think to mar,
But make – driving the soul from false to feal –
To thee, the reconciler, the one real,
In whom alone the *would be* and the *is* are met.

19.

Me thou hast given an infinite unrest,
A hunger – not at first after known good,
But something vague I knew not, and yet would –
The veiled Isis, thy will not understood;
A conscience tossing ever in my breast;
And something deeper, that will not be expressed,
Save as the Spirit thinking in the Spirit's brood.

6/16

I followed breadcrumb trails until the birds
Had eaten all. Night fell. In the dark wood
My hands stretched out before me, I heard words:
The valley of the shadow of death – good
Tree sound-waves steered me to a path of moss
And home. I'm freed by every painful loss;
You spin sheep fleece where once was milkweed floss.

6/17

Possess and Abandon, my mom and dad,
Gave me a head-start on a frozen heart.
Wandering Jews, the people of my race,
Taught me that here on earth I'd find no place.
When icy hearts are crushed by sin they start
To melt in that contrition beyond *bad*...
Where stream the living waters of God's grace.

6/18

I oft mistake that mocking demon for
My deep-down nature; capsized by this voice,
I drown in floods of second-guessing choice.
To hold a dream is as to have a door
Into the Dear – bliss beyond all outline –
There we in sweet quintessence thee adore!
There dance the bubble and the porcupine.

6/19

Sometimes thy Spirit-thoughts drop into gray
Matter, irrigating this thirsty brain;
Insight may grow and bloom within this rain,
Or stones be thrown up from the heart's earth, some may
Break the plow, be stumbling-blocks or key.
My tumult is to know what I must be:
Never enough in thanks, O Majesty!

20.

But now the Spirit and I are one in this –
My hunger now is after righteousness;
My spirit hopes in God to set me free
From the low self loathed of the higher me.
Great elder brother of my second birth,
Dear o'er all names but one, in heaven or earth,
Teach me all day to love eternally.

21.

Lo, Lord, thou know'st, I would not anything
That in the heart of God holds not its root;
Nor falsely deem there is any life at all
That doth in him nor sleep nor shine nor sing;
I know the plants that bear the noisome fruit
Of burning and of ashes and of gall –
From God's heart torn, rootless to man's they cling.

22.

Life-giving love rots to devouring fire;
Justice corrupts to despicable revenge;
Motherhood chokes in the dam's jealous mire;
Hunger for growth turns fluctuating change;
Love's anger grand grows spiteful human wrath,
Hunting men out of conscience' holy path;
And human kindness takes the tattler's range.

23.

Nothing can draw the heart of man but good;
Low good it is that draws him from the higher –
So evil – poison uncreate from food.
Never a foul thing, with temptation dire,
Tempts hellward force created to aspire,
But walks in wronged strength of imprisoned Truth,
Whose mantle also oft the Shame indu'th.

6/20

My earthly hungers thwarted, one by one –
Dare I aspire to righteousness when I
Am still in human grade school? Lightning sun,
Brother, char this self-loathing, let it die
Knowing even a low potato may
Print art or hold a beeswax candle. Day
After day, teach me to love and to pray.

6/21

Like *Le Pendu*, the hanged man, up-side-down,
We root in heaven and can bloom in Lent.
We who were wild, save for the golden rule,
Have much in common with a chastened fool.
Bound, smiling, tame, we rise/fall, one knee bent
In criss-cross 4, we pray in country/town,
For the will of God and a paper crown.

6/22

On this tightrope between renaissance and
Dilletante, each rare gift has its own flaw;
One moment dawn on eternity's sand,
The next a furnace in the dragon's jaw.
We may seek extremes as though these could keep
Us from sin. Where we must balance is steep,
High and narrow, precarious and deep.

6/23

Yes, good has oft been enemy of best.
Many a long detour have I taken
To love each fallen Lucifer, aghast
As one born yesterday to see my quest –
For Thee – dwindle to dead end. Forsaken
By illusions now, shamed, tied to thy mast,
I seek in thy heart refuge from my past.

24.

Love in the prime not yet I understand –
Scarce know the love that loveth at first hand:
Help me my selfishness to scatter and scout;
Blow on me till my love loves burningly;
Then the great love will burn the mean self out,
And I, in glorious simplicity,
Living by love, shall love unspeakably.

25.

Oh, make my anger pure – let no worst wrong
Rouse in me the old niggard selfishness.
Give me thine indignation – which is love
Turned on the evil that would part love's throng;
Thy anger scathes because it needs must bless,
Gathering into union calm and strong
All things on earth, and under, and above.

26.

Make my forgiveness downright – such as I
Should perish if I did not have from thee;
I let the wrong go, withered up and dry,
Cursed with divine forgetfulness in me.
'Tis but self-pity, pleasant, mean, and sly,
Low whispering bids the paltry memory live: –
What am I brother for, but to forgive!

27.

"Thou art my father's child – come to my heart:"
Thus must I say, or Thou must say, "Depart;"
Thus I would say – I would be as thou art;
Thus I must say, or still I work athwart
The absolute necessity and law
That dwells in me, and will me asunder draw,
If in obedience I leave any flaw.

6/24

I don't know how to love. Is it the bliss
Of slain-at-first-sight? Cupid's arrow? Or
That glimpse of God's Beyond? We long for more!
We must do the best we can, hit or miss.
Is it akin to pity? Who can say?
To live as widow or as fiancée –
Show my vocation – guide my lonely way.

6/25

My anger is most suspect; rides the flood
Of righteous indignation, carries freight
Of all unresolved grievances (and hate
May surface too thereby). Wash in thy blood
My arrogance, and by your holy rod
Raise me transfigured as a child of God,
That I within this grace may be Love's mate.

6/26

Let me forgive myself, Lord; it is time.
You have forgiven me, still I condemn
Myself as though cast out of the garden.
Perhaps contrition only dies when I'm
Completely able to receive *Je t'aime* –
Receive incomprehensible pardon
With Mary Magdalene, my paradigm.

6/27

Brothers and sisters, I am awfully shy,
But I aspire to trust before I die.
What true obedience is, I am not sure.
How should I know, whose motives are not pure?
My isolation near-complete: the eye
Of the chaotic hurricane is my
Quiet chapel. Solitude is thy cure.

28.

Lord, I forgive – and step in unto thee.
If I have enemies, Christ deal with them:
He hath forgiven me and Jerusalem.
Lord, set me from self-inspiration free,
And let me live and think from thee, not me –
Rather, from deepest me then think and feel,
At centre of thought's swift-revolving wheel.

29.

I sit o'ercanopied with Beauty's tent,
Through which flies many a golden-winged dove,
Well watched of Fancy's tender eyes up bent;
A hundred Powers wait on me, ministering;
A thousand treasures Art and Knowledge bring;
Will, Conscience, Reason tower the rest above;
But in the midst, alone, I gladness am and love.

30.

'Tis but a vision, Lord; I do not mean
That thus I am, or have one moment been –
'Tis but a picture hung upon my wall,
To measure dull contentment therewithal,
And know behind the human how I fall; –
A vision true, of what one day shall be,
When thou hast had thy very will with me.

6/28

Let orders from thy central Kingdom be
The impulse and redeeming of my life.
Especially may I forgive and care
For one who carved the cross that I must bear.
Since I am neither mother nor man's wife,
But clown and solitary, let me see
How my forgivenness may honor thee.

6/29

I sit surrounded by my family past,
Eating a pint of ice-cream, in deep-freeze.
My mother, ninety-two, is at once frail
And stubborn. How deep the divide, how vast –
The debris-tide, possessions, memories.
We sit in separate rooms; beyond our pale
Umbilical of mourning, joy will last.

6/30

As I was born, six million died in camps.
Hans Christian Andersen showed me a world
Where hope and justice lifted their bright lamps
In tales of sacrificial love. There, pearled,
I rose with Little Mermaid's pink-cloud foam,
Through family sorrow, by way of his poem,
Into the premonition of true Home.

JULY.

1.

ALAS, my tent! see through it a whirlwind sweep!
Moaning, poor Fancy's doves are swept away.
I sit alone, a sorrow half asleep,
My consciousness the blackness all astir.
No pilgrim I, a homeless wanderer –
For how canst Thou be in the darkness deep,
Who dwellest only in the living day?

2.

It must be, somewhere in my fluttering tent,
Strange creatures, half tamed only yet, are pent –
Dragons, lop-winged birds, and large-eyed snakes!
Hark! through the storm the saddest howling breaks!
Or are they loose, roaming about the bent,
The darkness dire deepening with moan and scream? –
My Morning, rise, and all shall be a dream.

3.

Not thine, my Lord, the darkness all is mine –
Save that, as mine, my darkness too is thine:
All things are thine to save or to destroy –
Destroy my darkness, rise my perfect joy;
Love primal, the live coal of every night,
Flame out, scare the ill things with radiant fright,
And fill my tent with laughing morn's delight.

JULY

7/1

I binge on sundaes by the shores of hell,
As though sheer weight, past gluttony, could save
Me from being ploughed under by each wave.
I listen not to cell phone but sea shell.
As "patriot" fireworks mass, I hear
(Through jet-booms, war-cries) "Float on, bubble dear –
Though martial gauntlet razorwires of fear."

7/2

My creatures do not leave with morning light.
Their anguish undermines my trust in thee.
Empathy for them makes me captive of
The desperate hungers they insist are love.
When duty cuts through mind's pathology,
And I engage in tasks, however slight,
The phantoms (minus me) are put to flight.

7/3

We see through a glass darkly. Lord, how dim
And cracked my vision is! Please let me know
In mausoleum dark that spark of hope
By which to see I am not doomed to mope
In this self-hating mirrored coffin – foe –
Afraid to love. Alone. Through, with, in Him,
Prune or make bud for good this crooked limb!

4.

Master, thou workest with such common things—
Low souls, weak hearts, I mean – and hast to use,
Therefore, such common means and rescuings,
That hard we find it, as we sit and muse,
To think thou workest in us verily:
Bad sea-boats we, and manned with wretched crews –
That doubt the captain, watch the storm-spray flee.

5.

Thou art hampered in thy natural working then
When beings designed on freedom's holy plan
Will not be free: with thy poor, foolish men,
Thou therefore hast to work just like a man.
But when, tangling thyself in their sore need,
Thou hast to freedom fashioned them indeed,
Then wilt thou grandly move, and Godlike speed.

6.

Will this not then show grandest fact of all –
In thy creation victory most renowned –
That thou hast wrought thy will by slow and small,
And made men like thee, though thy making bound
By that which they were not, and could not be
Until thou mad'st them make along with thee? –
Master, the tardiness is but in me.

7.

Hence come thy checks – because I still would run
My head into the sand, nor flutter aloft
Towards thy home, with thy wind under me.
'Tis because I am mean, thy ways so oft
Look mean to me; my rise is low begun;
But scarce thy will doth grasp me, ere I see,
For my arrest and rise, its stern necessity.

7/4

This peaceful day, the inland butterflies –
On lobelia (regatta marine blue)
And white snapdragon – sail the summer breeze.
The pond is green with reeds and leafy trees.
Profoundest gratitude rings humble-true.
The air is sweet with wildflowers and birdcries;
An ant walks on barnwood beneath thy skies.

7/5

O, fashion me to freedom, Lord, and soon!
This rolling stone seeks each day her new bond.
Rich moss to anchor in beneath thy moon,
Deep roots to unfurl from like ferny frond.
I wash my nomad car and then it rains,
Seek direction from iron weathervanes.
Shall I stay put, or lift off with the cranes?

7/6

Dear Lord, hoodwinked and being chipped away
'Till there be nothing left but farewell tears,
The fountain both of gratitude and grief;
My heart is gone, and well I know the thief.
Little by little, always in arrears;
Opinions, ideas, certainties – all prey
To thy exquisite chisel this new day.

7/7

The term "severe mercy" is so exact.
When wisdom and intuition marry
At intersection of thy holy cross,
The letting-go-forgiving-painful-loss
(Bench-press weight we give to thee to carry)
Leaves us renewed/transformed, and fresh/intact,
Cleansed of illusion, yet set free from fact.

8.

Like clogs upon the pinions of thy plan
We hang – like captives on thy chariot-wheels,
Who should climb up and ride with Death's conqueror;
Therefore thy train along the world's highway teals
So slow to the peace of heart-reluctant man.
What shall we do to spread the wing and soar,
Nor straiten thy deliverance any more?

9.

The sole way to put flight into the wing,
To preen its feathers, and to make them grow,
Is to heed humbly every smallest thing
With which the Christ in us has aught to do.
So will the Christ from child to manhood go,
Obedient to the father Christ, and so
Sweet holy change will turn all our old things to new.

10.

Creation thou dost work by faint degrees,
By shade and shadow from unseen beginning;
Far, far apart, in unthought mysteries
Of thy own dark, unfathomable seas,
Thou will'st thy will; and thence, upon the earth –
Slow travelling, his way through centuries winning –
A child at length arrives at never ending birth.

11.

Well mayst thou then work on indocile hearts
By small successes, disappointments small;
By nature, weather, failure, or sore fall;
By shame, anxiety, bitterness, and smarts;
By loneliness, by weary loss of zest: –
The rags, the husks, the swine, the hunger-quest,
Drive home the wanderer to the father's breast.

7/8

Like children on the brink of growing pains
We play (it is our work) with thy great toys,
Imagining ourselves both brave and strong
Before we risk eternal transport trains.
Wait for us slowpokes, for the girls and boys
Who practice flight at first with paper planes,
May circle zodiacs in nursery song.

7/9

Turn, turn, turn, through the seasons and the song;
The tiny grains of beach sand from hard rock
Sift, precious moments, hours dark and bright.
The wind stirs in seashell ears as ere long
We hear thy still, small voice beyond the clock,
Within temptation. Psyche's tasks are light –
We hear, are fed; we do, and we take flight!

7/10

O, may we neverendingly live, grow
Through and beyond the errors of our days,
That even these old branches, pruned and bent,
May bud into new greenings, sweet and slow.
After hard rains, crushed blossoms heaven-scent
The air with forgiveness, and with this praise-
Hope balanced we walk tightrope in thy ways.

7/11

Let us not drift in orbit 'round the stars,
Beyond the union of Venus and Mars.
Our lives on Vulcan's anvil we submit:
Suffering/joyful, iron from the clay,
Grown into truths we cannot yet admit;
Let us be grateful prodigals, dare say –
We too may enter heaven's gate one day.

12.

How suddenly some rapid turn of thought
May throw the life-machine all out of gear,
Clouding the windows with the steam of doubt,
Filling the eyes with dust, with noise the ear!
Who knows not then where dwells the engineer,
Rushes aghast into the pathless night,
And wanders in a land of dreary fright.

13.

Amazed at sightless whirring of their wheels,
Confounded with the recklessness and strife,
Distract with fears of what may next ensue,
Some break rude exit from the house of life,
And plunge into a silence out of view –
Whence not a cry, no wafture once reveals
What door they have broke open with the knife.

14.

Help me, my Father, in whatever dismay,
Whatever terror in whatever shape,
To hold the faster by thy garment's hem;
When my heart sinks, oh, lift it up, I pray;
Thy child should never fear though hell should gape,
Not blench though all the ills that men affray
Stood round him like the Romans round Jerusalem.

15.

Too eager I must not be to understand.
How should the work the master goes about
Fit the vague sketch my compasses have planned?
I am his house – for him to go in and out.
He builds me now – and if I cannot see
At any time what he is doing with me,
'Tis that he makes the house for me too grand.

7/12

Those of us born into the temple Doubt,
(There, orthodoxy murders baby faith
With common sense and intellect/despair),
At home in pathless night, may see as wraith
Too diamond-brilliant thy light shining out!
For that old life sit *shiva*, garments tear,
And all the courage of new blindness wear.

7/13

Like suicides caught up in gears of clocks,
Or in the squirrel-cage of our own mind,
We violently enter our own hearts,
And eat them out 'till nothing's left but rind.
A troglodyte within a bone-cart box,
Assailed by memories and missing parts:
Then come the angel, eagle, lion, ox!

7/14

Carry me, Lord, when the tiny things scare,
(Panicked confusions and gnat clouds that sting).
My tears on thy neck – I worry, I sigh –
Closer and closer to thee I must cling.
Help me this cowardly nature to bear,
Help me to see the moon rise in the sky,
And to hear human hearts beating nearby.

7/15

I have no sketch, no expectation now.
What good there may be in my being I
Can never see; my flaws I see too clear,
And these discourage me. O speed the plough,
That these grim weeds may shrivel up and die
Without uprooting the few virtues here.
Guide me in right formation, Lord Most High.

16.

The house is not for me – it is for him.
His royal thoughts require many a stair,
Many a tower, many an outlook fair,
Of which I have no thought, and need no care.
Where I am most perplexed, it may be there
Thou mak'st a secret chamber, holy-dim,
Where thou wilt come to help my deepest prayer.

17.

I cannot tell why this day I am ill;
But I am well because it is thy will –
Which is to make me pure and right like thee.
Not yet I need escape – 'tis bearable
Because thou knowest. And when harder things
Shall rise and gather, and overshadow me,
I shall have comfort in thy strengthenings.

18.

How do I live when thou art far away? –
When I am sunk, and lost, and dead in sleep,
Or in some dream with no sense in its play?
When weary-dull, or drowned in study deep? –
O Lord, I live so utterly on thee,
I live when I forget thee utterly –
Not that thou thinkest of, but thinkest me.

19.

Thou far! – that word the holy truth doth blur.
Doth the great ocean from the small fish run
When it sleeps fast in its low weedy bower?
Is the sun far from any smallest flower,
That lives by his dear presence every hour?
Are they not one in oneness without stir –
The flower the flower because the sun the sun?

7/16

My life is not my own, it is thy green:
Whether I have sense/being yet or no,
Whether of weed or wheat I have no clue,
Or palm beneath thy donkey's foot. I go
On growing in this husk, unseeing, seen
(Though wild, I trust) and heard (I hope) by you
Who winnow me until I can come clean.

7/17

This day I have no breath to pray at all.
I cannot much reflect when I am sick,
Even when well, I am not truly sure:
Is this thy will? Am I right, good and pure?
To breathe eternal love would be my cure.
May each beat of my heart be prayer call.
Hear me, dear Lord – you know what makes me tick.

7/18

Small squabbles over nothing raise the blue
Spectre of anticipatory grief.
It rains – my tears are overflowing too.
Here's breakfast, with the raisins and oatmeal
Humble in the bowl. *Thanksgiving*. This brief
Instant is mine. Grace and peace set their seal
Of infinite love upon me – keen, real.

7/19

This morning in a caul of care and stress
(Within the bright perfection of the day),
Assailed from deep within by fear of change,
Confused by every *no* that meets my *yes*,
Perplexed: Lord, shall I go or shall I stay?
Conflicting wisdoms through my brainfield range.
Where is serenity? Help me to pray!

20.

"Dear presence every hour"! – what of the night,
When crumpled daisies shut gold sadness in;
And some do hang the head for lack of light,
Sick almost unto death with absence-blight? –
Thy memory then, warm-lingering in the ground,
Mourned dewy in the air, keeps their hearts sound,
Till fresh with day their lapsed life begin.

21.

All things are shadows of the shining true:
Sun, sea, and air – close, potent, hurtless fire –
Flowers from their mother's prison-dove, and dew –
Every thing holds a slender guiding clue
Back to the mighty oneness: – hearts of faith
Know thee than light, than heat, endlessly nigher,
Our life's life, carpenter of Nazareth.

22.

Sometimes, perhaps, the spiritual blood runs slow,
And soft along the veins of will doth flow,
Seeking God's arteries from which it came.
Or does the etherial, creative flame
Turn back upon itself, and latent grow? –
It matters not what figure or what name,
If thou art in me, and I am not to blame.

23.

In such God-silence, the soul's nest, so long
As all is still, no flutter and no song,
Is safe. But if my soul begin to act
Without some waking to the eternal fact
That my dear life is hid with Christ in God –
I think and move a creature of earth's clod,
Stand on the finite, act upon the wrong.

7/20

Don Juan, my priest, says we'll meet in heaven.
He says this to all women he will woo.
My mother in the choir-loft trusts no God.
Her name is Daisy, fresh fading leaven.
Her orthodoxy says she'll die a Jew.
I mourn. I share mystic conversions odd;
Believe all pilgrim roads will lead to you.

7/21

Lord, let me know I have a place in thee!
Am I nun, old maid, spry little lady,
Rapunzel in tower? I live and learn;
My bloom pricks my mother – what's to be done?
Help me to act (if it be thy will) *turn,*
Turn, turn – thy bounty is too much for me!
How can I seek a home when Christ had none?

7/22

I read of missionaries in far lands,
While parsing small decisions every day.
My poverty of faith could not be more;
Even on shallows' shore I feel quicksands.
Safe in the lukewarm, far from savage war,
Stowaway renter, fearing to own; may
You draw me to you, Lord, within this fray.

7/23

In such God-silence (by traffic noise scored)
Far beneath the waves, deep down in the sea,
Bracketed by birdsong, my soul must part
To know herself at one in thy great heart.
All of our partings reunite in thee.
To turn away from love is to go toward:
I understand the meaning of m'lord.

24.

My soul this sermon hence for itself prepares: –
"Then is there nothing vile thou mayst not do,
Buffeted in a tumult of low cares,
And treacheries of the old man 'gainst the new."–
Lord, in my spirit let thy spirit move,
Warning, that it may not have to reprove: –
In my dead moments, master, stir the prayers.

25.

Lord, let my soul o'erburdened then feel thee
Thrilling through all its brain's stupidity.
If I must slumber, heedless of ill harms,
Let it not be but in my Father's arms;
Outside the shelter of his garment's fold,
All is a waste, a terror-haunted wold. –
Lord, keep me. 'Tis thy child that cries. Behold.

26.

Some say that thou their endless love hast won
By deeds for them which I may not believe
Thou ever didst, or ever willedst done:
What matter, so they love thee? They receive
Eternal more than the poor loom and wheel
Of their invention ever wove and spun. –
I love thee for I must, thine all from head to heel.

27.

The love of thee will set all notions right.
Right save by love no thought can be or may;
Only love's knowledge is the primal light.
Questions keep camp along love's shining coast –
Challenge my love and would my entrance stay:
Across the buzzing, doubting, challenging host,
I rush to thee, and cling, and cry – *Thou know'st.*

7/24

Let me not swap my earthly love for thee,
Nor put him in thy place to worship dear.
Keep me discerning, but don't let my life
Be living death-by-scrupulosity.
Let me know joy as well as worthy strife.
Please guide my actions through the gauntlet fear;
This widow/fiancée sings, "Be thou near!"

7/25

Rest in thy arms? Lord, what a lovely way!
I never knew that. Once, in Lincoln Park,
Mother lifted me up into the lap
Of the statue monument, cold, hard, dark.
I beg (who hugged tree-trunks and thought love sap,
Seeking the father's heart within the bark):
"Hold me, this Christmas-in-July, all day."

7/26

I know joy is from thee, who cracked the shell
Of hard-boiled sorrow in my brain-cooked hell.
Embarrassments of riches are revealed –
The tiny cottage and the green farm field,
Eternal love ongoing, sacred heart,
All part and parcel of thy healing art;
Peace, grace, reunion – stone moved, tomb unsealed!

7/27

Most lovely liturgical music plays
On the radio, thick with static woes;
A French station wanders in for a while,
Then out again. The heron comes and goes.
Silence. Cars, birds and chipmunks sing their lays.
I worry, tear flesh, as the heartbeat prays
Deep in the chapel of seeking/exile.

28.

Oh, let me live in thy realities,
Nor substitute my notions for thy facts,
Notion with notion making leagues and pacts;
They are to truth but as dream-deeds to acts,
And questioned, make me doubt of everything. –
"O Lord, my God," my heart gets up and cries,
"Come thy own self, and with thee my faith bring."

29.

O master, my desires to work, to know,
To be aware that I do live and grow –
All restless wish for anything not thee,
I yield, and on thy altar offer me.
Let me no more from out thy presence go,
But keep me waiting watchful for thy will –
Even while I do it, waiting watchful still.

30.

Thou art the Lord of life, the secret thing.
Thou wilt give endless more than I could find,
Even if without thee I could go and seek;
For thou art one, Christ, with my deepest mind,
Duty alive, self-willed, in me dost speak,
And to a deeper purer being sting:
I come to thee, my life, my causing kind.

31.

Nothing is alien in thy world immense –
No look of sky or earth or man or beast;
"In the great hand of God I stand, and thence"
Look out on life, his endless, holy feast.
To try to feel is but to court despair,
To dig for a sun within a garden-fence:
Who does thy will, O God, he lives upon thy air.

7/28

Dear Lord, I have begun so late to act,
Not just react. I still ask air, "May I?"
In the game where we take baby paces
But first must ask. Even when passing by
The pepper for salt, I fear in fact
To slight pepper. Please, give me thy graces
To risk as well as to obey, Most High.

7/29

Yes, Lord – take me entirely (good/bad)
Upon thy justice-mercy seat (sane/mad).
Let me be recollected, hopeful, still –
To wait and watch and know and do thy will.
Touch me, enroll me (bitter/dumbstruck/sweet)
In the *yeshiva* at thy punctured feet,
Braiding the weeds, and raising up the wheat!

7/30

Thou art the Lord of home, the secret place,
The reconcilliation and the rest,
The fountain that o'erflows my narrow banks.
Father, beyond all telling you have blessed
Me with beatitudes; I give thee thanks!
Though in my life I walk the tortoise-race,
Thy kingdom come – help me tell good from best.

7/31

I'll make my fence of sunshine so's to keep
Temptations out while radiating light
You lend me through the clouds of troubled sleep,
Or waves of changing feelings. Like a kite
Anchored in earth, I ride the wind of grace
And hope that what's renounced here finds its place
To root and bloom beyond this time and space.

AUGUST.

1.

SO shall abundant entrance me be given
Into the truth, my life's inheritance.
Lo! as the sun shoots straight from out his tomb,
God-floated, casting round a lordly glance
Into the corners of his endless room,
So, through the rent which thou, O Christ, hast riven,
I enter liberty's divine expanse.

2.

It will be so – ah, so it is not now!
Who seeks thee for a little lazy peace,
Then, like a man all weary of the plough,
That leaves it standing in the furrow's crease,
Turns from thy presence for a foolish while,
Till comes again the rasp of unrest's file,
From liberty is distant many a mile.

3.

Like one that stops, and drinks, and turns, and goes
Into a land where never water flows,
There travels on, the dry and thirsty day,
Until the hot night veils the farther way,
Then turns and finds again the bubbling pool –
Here would I build my house, take up my stay,
Nor ever leave my Sychar's margin cool.

AUGUST

8/1

The tomb is open! We can either spoil,
Or lift our shrouded heads above the soil,
Refreshed by rain or warmed by brilliant sky,
Born from the pierced Godheart's entreating cry.
We heed an invitation from above
To enter into freedom, past slave-coil,
And seek to be participants in Love.

8/2

"In work is liberty" – even in prayers?
This lie gave hope to inmates in death-camp.
Each day a small verse, never being sure
Whether (like tears upon a rock) the layers
Of sediment sparkle under the lamp
You light to guide our little steps. May pure
Love-being (not just doing) bring our cure.

8/3

Late afternoon, I come to Jacob's well,
Where upright women come at break of day.
There, stranger-God-love tells me who I am!
He speaks to *me*, an outcast/long-lost lamb,
To say he is – *Messiah!* Do I stay,
Give him a cup to drink, or run to tell
Who gave me living water in my hell?

4.

Keep me, Lord, with thee. I call from out the dark –
Hear in thy light, of which I am a spark.
I know not what is mine and what is thine –
Of branch and stem I miss the differing mark –
But if a mere hair's-breadth me separateth,
That hair's-breadth is eternal, infinite death.
For sap thy dead branch calls, O living vine!

5.

I have no choice, I must do what I can;
But thou dost me, and all things else as well;
Thou wilt take care thy child shall grow a man.
Rouse thee, my faith; be king; with life be one;
To trust in God is action's highest kind;
Who trusts in God, his heart with life doth swell;
Faith opens all the windows to God's wind.

6.

O Father, thou art my eternity.
Not on the clasp of consciousness – on thee
My life depends; and I can well afford
All to forget, so thou remember, Lord.
In thee I rest; in sleep thou dost me fold;
In thee I labour; still in thee, grow old;
And dying, shall I not in thee, my Life, be bold?

7.

In holy things may be unholy greed.
Thou giv'st a glimpse of many a lovely thing,
Not to be stored for use in any mind,
But only for the present spiritual need.
The holiest bread, if hoarded, soon will breed
The mammon-moth, the having-pride, I find.
'Tis momently thy heart gives out heart-quickening.

8/4

"Rain may be heavy at times": this warning
From an announcer drowned out by storm sound.
Wildfires in the west seem so surreal.
This weather's fog-mist of longterm mourning
Threatens to damp the spark of love we feel.
Beyond feeling, let us know we are found
Worthy to touch thy hem and dog thy heel.

8/5

I have a choice and will stay in the mold
You fashioned for my soul when it was old.
I must be true to thee despite how dumb
And solitaire and hard to bear I be.
I do believe you'll make a woman from
The wounded teen-child elder that I see,
And trust you'll give me faith to yield to thee.

8/6

I am not bold – death is a mystery,
To live a-right is courage-grace to me.
Another church is breaking from within,
Discerning earnestly the face of sin.
How we may love ourselves, and how love thee
Before we die is what concerns me most.
If you don't help us, good Lord, we are toast!

8/7

Just now *Prince Igor* plays – this haunting poem
Fills me with joy. I stand in moments rare,
A super on the opera stage, in bliss,
As be-wigged maidens sing of missing home,
And fake snowflakes drift slowly down the air
Thrilling with choral music. Times like this
Of holy poverty we gladly bear!

8.

It is thyself, and neither this nor that,
Nor anything, told, taught, or dreamed of thee,
That keeps us live. The holy maid who sat
Low at thy feet, choosing the better part,
Rising, bore with her – what a memory!
Yet, brooding only on that treasure, she
Had soon been roused by conscious loss of heart.

9.

I am a fool when I would stop and think,
And lest I lose my thoughts, from duty shrink.
It is but avarice in another shape.
'Tis as the vine-branch were to hoard the grape,
Nor trust the living root beneath the sod.
What trouble is that child to thee, my God,
Who sips thy gracious cup, and will not drink!

10.

True, faithful action only is the life,
The grapes for which we feel the pruning knife.
Thoughts are but leaves; they fall and feed the ground.
The holy seasons, swift and slow, go round;
The ministering leaves return, fresh, large, and rife –
But fresher, larger, more thoughts to the brain: –
Farewell, my dove! – come back, hope-laden, through the rain.

11.

Well may this body poorer, feebler grow!
It is undressing for its last sweet bed;
But why should the soul, which death shall never know,
Authority, and power, and memory shed?
It is that love with absolute faith would wed;
God takes the inmost garments off his child,
To have him in his arms, naked and undefiled.

8/8

Like students, taking notes all day, we try
To press an essence between Bible leaves,
Hold flat rose petals up to sunset light,
Search proofs while missing pink clouds in the sky.
Mary keeps thy words deep in her heart – bright
Evanescent mysteries – as the sheaves
Are gathered, praise in each small cricket cry.

8/9

In John you take sour vinegar/strong mint.
Some do not drink, euphoric madness fear –
Can only sip ambrosia in a tear.
In sieve-minds thoughts run misty, shapeshift – flee.
Let us commune with you by grace and dint
Of duty's tasks, that at this instant we
May drink the hyssop sponge of thine and thee.

8/10

It is right hard to let the loved one go
In order to obey commandments great.
Renunciation mulch is quite the best,
Hold close with open arms ongoing quest.
The new world lies through death itself and so
(Luke twenty-two:eighteen) grape's pressing fate –
To be Lord's Pesach mead at heaven's gate.

8/11

Aging as ongoing creation! Such
A way of seeing must have cost so much.
As husk and fragrant tassel close the corn
Called "synagogue" by Dylan Thomas, so
Chrisms for the elders soon-to-be-born,
Annointing tears, love's grief as we let go;
Death bright as prism star in God's new morn.

12.

Thou art my knowledge and my memory,
No less than my real, deeper life, my love.
I will not fool, degrade myself to trust
In less than that which maketh me say Me,
In less than that causing itself to be.
Thou art within me, behind, beneath, above –
I will be thine because I may and must.

13.

Thou art the truth, the life. Thou, Lord, wilt see
To every question that perplexes me.
I am thy being; and my dignity
Is written with my name down in thy book;
Thou wilt care for it. Never shall I think
Of anything that thou mightst overlook: –
In faith-born triumph at thy feet I sink.

14.

Thou carest more for that which I call mine,
In same sort-better manner than I could,
Even if I knew creation's ends divine,
Rousing in me this vague desire of good.
Thou art more to me than my desires' whole brood;
Thou art the only person, and I cry
Unto the father *I* of this my *I*.

15.

Thou who inspirest prayer, then bend'st thine ear;
Its crying with love's grand respect to hear!
I cannot give myself to thee aright –
With the triumphant uttermost of gift;
That cannot be till I am full of light–
To perfect deed a perfect will must lift: –
Inspire, possess, compel me, first of every might.

8/12

I know I've been much too slow to amend
My human nature that encloses thee.
I fear the imperfections of the mold
Obscure the message you may send in me.
May I be evidently thine; more bend,
Be more forgiving, kind to foe and friend,
Not least the foe within – the deaf, the cold.

8/13

Here in the small town, at the County Fair,
Far from wars/cities/sorrows of our race,
Thy presence shines in the eye of each cow!
I walk in bliss, astonished by thy grace,
Among the farm-folk, marveling at how
Thy ark, infinite, present everywhere –
Lifts 'till I literally float on air.

8/14

I have small "i"; am just approaching "mine",
Cautiously choosing only broken things
To save, redeem and mend – thus dare to own,
So imitating you, who are a sign
To lost ones that Icarus' wax wings
Begin an ascent in which hope is sown,
As we fall into thee, our sea divine.

8/15

Good, best and perfect – how can we aspire
Unless you comfort us when we fall short?
Lest we lose heart, help us to start anew,
Regress, attempt, grow braver, truer blue.
Here, bringing up the rear, we see the fire!
We dare not think of justice-mercy court –
Guide every step, dear Lord, we've only you!

16.

I do not wonder men can ill believe
Who make poor claims upon thee, perfect Lord;
Then most I trust when most I would receive.
I wonder not that such do pray and grieve –
The God they think, to be God is not fit.
Then only in thy glory I seem to sit,
When my heart claims from thine an infinite accord.

17.

More life I need ere I myself can be.
Sometimes, when the eternal tide ebbs low,
A moment weary of my life I grow –
Weary of my existence' self, I mean,
Not of its plodding, not its wind and snow
Then to thy knee trusting I turn, and lean:
Thou will'st I live, and I do will with thee.

18.

Dost thou mean sometimes that we should forget thee,
Dropping the veil of things 'twixt thee and us? –
Ah, not that we should lose thee and regret thee!
But that, we turning from our windows thus,
The frost-fixed God should vanish from the pane,
Sun-melted, and a moment, Father, let thee
Look like thyself straight into heart and brain.

19.

For sometimes when I am busy among men,
With heart and brain an open thoroughfare
For faces, words, and thoughts other than mine,
And a pause comes at length – oh, sudden then,
Back throbs the tide with rush exultant rare;
And for a gentle moment I divine
Thy dawning presence flush my tremulous air.

8/16

As Martha seeks a hand with heirloom plate,
Mary's heart-manna is Word, as his great,
Harmonious peace is conceived/descends –
Transforming rabbi's servants into friends,
Death into life, hearthfire to holy ghost.
Perhaps our bridegroom at the sisters' roast
Is changing even now from guest to Host!

8/17

To live this gift-life, I must work to shed
All aids to otherforce which wants me dead.
The small right actions which comprise each day
Run gauntlet through a chaos roundelay,
Both in and out; I fight through powers'-veil
And principalities beyond the pale –
Absurd or sturdy – following thy Way.

8/18

In reaching out to trust, I am hemmed in
By human longing I perceive as sin.
The stomach-intuition and the brain
Confirm my way as would a dowser's cane.
When disappointments seem my only kin,
And I am lost again, or set apart –
Then shall I hear thee beating in my heart.

8/19

Even here on the outskirts of the world,
The wind of holy spirit blows right through
The tattered, permeated fencing shreds.
Sheep of insomnia, their bellies pearled,
Evaporate in morning's ghostly dew.
As August and September, newlyweds,
Drift into union, Lord: I call on you!

20.

If I have to forget thee, do thou see
It be a good, not bad forgetfulness;
That all its mellow, truthful air be free
From dusty *noes*, and soft with many a *yes*;
That as thy breath my life, my life may be
Man's breath. So when thou com'st at hour unknown,
Thou shalt find nothing in me but thine own.

21.

Thou being in me, in my deepest me,
Through all the time I do not think of thee,
Shall I not grow at last so true within
As to forget thee and yet never sin?
Shall I not walk the loud world's busy way,
Yet in thy palace-porch sit all the day?
Not conscious think of thee, yet never from thee stray?

22.

Forget! – Oh, must it be? – Would it were rather
That every sense was so filled with my father
That not in anything could I forget him,
But deepest, highest must in all things set him! –
Yet if thou think in me, God, what great matter
Though my poor thought to former break and latter –
As now my best thoughts; break, before thee foiled, and scatter!

23.

Some way there must be of my not forgetting,
And thither thou art leading me, my God.
The child that, weary of his mother's petting,
Runs out the moment that his feet are shod,
May see her face in every flower he sees,
And she, although beyond the window sitting,
Be nearer him than when he sat upon her knees.

8/20

As God breathes into Old Soul become breeze,
The *Ruach* where the six-winged seraph flies –
(We asthma-folk know breath is godly gift;
A small dust mote may bring us to our knees) –
May Holy Spirit fill us, kind and swift,
That as we exhale praise our sorrows lift
And we take inspiration each sunrise.

8/21

As when the spoken prayer moves to the heart
That beats in thee beyond the farthest stars,
When we be spirit (beyond Adam's bone,
New-flesh of tears and longing, singing stone)
Words fail immaculately. Heavens part –
We see through mayhem (trusting, knowing, known) –
Thy full moon move to shield the world from Mars.

8/22

Lord, you yourself broke in unleavened bread,
Snapped Sabbath wheat-heads with divinity:
Things shatter when thy will-force hits us hard –
Both cosmic eggs and shroud-clothes of the dead.
Crucified/risen, holy Trinity,
Your blood sweet in cracked chalice; essence, nard –
And pearl of great price in a seashell shard!

8/23

The birdseed-grass that hides the baby mole
(Who last night was my old cat's favorite prey
Till I heard urgent squeak and rushed to save)
Is as sweet/green a refuge as this day.
To know thee is the purpose of each soul.
Can mind forget its maker when the wave
Of *recognition* rolls along the way?

24.

What if, when I at last, at the long last,
Shall see thy face, my Lord, my life's delight,
It should not be the face that hath been glassed
In poor imagination's mirror slight!
Will my soul sink, and shall I stand aghast,
Beggared of hope, my heart a conscious blight,
Amazed and lost—death's bitterness come and not passed?

25.

Ah, no! for from thy heart the love will press,
And shining from thy perfect human face,
Will sink into me like the father's kiss;
And deepening wide the gulf of consciousness
Beyond imagination's lowest abyss,
Will, with the potency of creative grace,
Lord it throughout the larger thinking place.

26.

Thus God-possessed, new born, ah, not for long
Should I the sight behold, beatified,
Know it creating in me, feel the throng
Of speechless hopes out-throbbing like a tide,
And my heart rushing, borne aloft the flood,
To offer at his feet its living blood –
Ere, glory-hid, the other face I spied.

27.

For our imagination is, in small,
And with the making-difference that must be,
Mirror of God's creating mirror; all
That shows itself therein, that formeth he,
And there is Christ, no bodiless vanity,
Though, face to face, the mighty perfectness
With glory blurs the dim-reflected less.

8/24

What if we stopped at icon's devout line,
Rather than sought a window into light
Itself? I can't imagine God at all.
The painter's faith may lead me past design
Out of the bitterness of my own night,
Into the Father's house beyond death's wall
Incomprehensible, the unknown All.

8/25

When intuition brings me to my knees,
Or kinship of the cat, or call of geese,
I travel in, beyond all time and space –
How can I look up so far as thy face?
I rise in living love and growing peace.
The convert school unspools such mysteries –
Yearned prayers answered by the light of grace.

8/26

Ah, twin begettings, harnessed by the breeze.
Longing to seize and give all good we hold,
Having been cracked, a brightful harvest, bold
In autumn prophesies in amber, gold.
Looking through windows, or in mirrors, please
Gentle the falling of each fragile grief
Into the perfect pond of true belief.

8/27

In hospital on this glorious day –
I'm (ministered to by stranger and friend)
So grateful! Children, take the jump-rope end,
And in the sacred spiral of the play,
Call forth in seashell, shard and grateful song,
The love of him to whom we all belong,
Just now as loss and hope so sweetly blend!

28.

I clasp thy feet, O father of the living!
Thou wilt not let my fluttering hopes be more,
Or lovelier, or greater, than thy giving!
Surely thy ships will bring to my poor shore,
Of gold and peacocks such a shining store
As will laugh all the dreams to holy scorn,
Of love and sorrow that were ever born.

29.

Sometimes it seems pure natural to trust,
And trust right largely, grandly, infinitely,
Daring the splendour of the giver's part;
At other times, the whole earth is but dust,
The sky is dust, yea, dust the human heart;
Then art thou nowhere, there is no room for thee
In the great dust-heap of eternity.

30.

But why should it be possible to mistrust –
Nor possible only, but its opposite hard?
Why should not man believe because he must –
By sight's compulsion? Why should he be scarred
With conflict? worn with doubting fine and long? –
No man is fit for heaven's musician throng
Who has not tuned an instrument all shook and jarred.

31.

Therefore, O Lord, when all things common seem,
When all is dust, and self the centre clod,
When grandeur is a hopeless, foolish dream,
And anxious care more reasonable than God, –
Out of the ashes I will call to thee –
In spite of dead distrust call earnestly: –
Oh thou who livest, call, then answer dying me.

8/28

Because the living water o'erfloods
The holy feet of God the poet-son
Whose own loved Father blesses/loves him true,
We share this immortality, we too!
Nothing may be possessed. When life is done,
Lightspirit glimmerings, last-rose fragrant bloods
Merge in the Godheart, raining holy dew!

8/29

After the ovens, it seemed mad to trust.
When victims take up arms, we too oppress.
World without end, we weep and call on thee –
In every language man shapes thought to be –
Call on the Mercy, beg for love's redress!
Lord, wed us instantly to "enemy";
Consumate, sanctify, and make us just.

8/30

Holding gospel music, a bit timeworn,
I walk in baby steps a tune unknown -
Forgiven, loved, and welcomed at the feast,
Awed by the vast, celestial chorus zone,
As by my hair's-breath escape from the beast;
Finding the one white rose without a thorn,
Safe in the alto section, faith reborn.

8/31

Darling MacDonald, sorrow (music, art,
Psalm and response in each cathedral heart;
Grief-praises, *ashes, ashes* ecstasy)
Paves August's way into month number nine.
We living now call, hear, and answer thee:
Thanks for good seed, for sowing strife divine –
This harvest is entirely from thine!

SEPTEMBER.

1.

WE are a shadow and a shining, we!
One moment nothing seems but what we see,
Nor aught to rule but common circumstance –
Nought is to seek but praise, to shun but chance;
A moment more, and God is all in all,
And not a sparrow from its nest can fall
But from the ground its chirp goes up into his hall.

2.

I know at least which is the better mood.
When on a heap of cares I sit and brood,
Like Job upon his ashes, sorely vext,
I feel a lower thing than when I stood
The world's true heir, fearless as, on its stalk,
A lily meeting Jesus in his walk:
I am not all mood – I can judge betwixt.

3.

Such differing moods can scarce to one belong;
Shall the same fountain sweet and bitter yield?
Shall what bore late the dust-mood, think and brood
Till it bring forth the great believing mood?
Or that which bore the grand mood, bald and peeled,
Sit down to croon the shabby sensual song,
To hug itself, and sink from wrong to meaner wrong?

SEPTEMBER

9/1

We are a shining host of children, we!
One moment earthbound, awkward, off-key sing,
Prisoned in bodies, foibles, memory-strewn –
Drying in time's air from the plum to prune –
The next, on incandescent kindly acts
We float in paradises far from tracts,
Within our Lord – these gratitudes we bring!

9/2

Comatose/spent, pierced by crow-caws absurd –
Percussions of kingfishers, each wet leaf,
In still air after all-night driving rain.
The medications warp my calm belief,
Manic emotion-thoughts rocket the brain.
Here on thy palm, Lord, I, thy homing bird –
Let go all else to hear thy guiding word.

9/3

Incomprehensible beatitudes
Shower me; beyond knowing all is well.
I choose once more to receive life in bloom:
This day – again – God opens every tomb!
Here in the gratitude beyond all moods,
First quarter of the Harvest Moon, we tell,
Rejoicing, how far we have come from hell!

4.

In the low mood, the mere man acts alone,
Moved by impulses which, if from within,
Yet far outside the centre man begin;
But in the grand mood, every softest tone
Comes from the living God at very heart –
From thee who infinite core of being art,
Thee who didst call our names ere ever we could sin.

5.

There is a coward sparing in the heart,
Offspring of penury and low-born fear: –
Prayer must take heed nor overdo its part,
Asking too much of him with open ear!
Sinners must wait, not seek the very best,
Cry out for peace, and be of middling cheer: –
False heart! thou cheatest God, and dost thy life molest.

6.

Thou hungerest not, thou thirstest not enough.
Thou art a temporizing thing, mean heart.
Down-drawn, thou pick'st up straws and wretched stuff,
Stooping as if the world's floor were the chart
Of the long way thy lazy feet must tread.
Thou dreamest of the crown hung o'er thy head –
But that is safe – thou gatherest hairs and fluff!

7.

Man's highest action is to reach up higher,
Stir up himself to take hold of his sire.
Then best I love you, dearest, when I go
And cry to love's life I may love you so
As to content the yearning, making love,
That perfects strength divine in weakness' fire,
And from the broken pots calls out the silver dove.

9/4

The sun shines through this paradise on earth.
Complete surrender, muted in a cloud,
Transports us into yet another day.
We move in witness with a blesséd crowd,
Both here/beyond at once – we love and pray,
In God's heart/beat/breath past all words can say –
Ongoing resurrections into birth.

9/5

Often it's hard for sinners to believe
Ourselves forgiven – such mercy/so much!
So we may seek to touch his lowest hem;
Not even dare to throw away the crutch.
Habits of being were old root and stem –
Now we new-bloom, such outworn chaff we leave –
And ask for more, and *all*, by grace receive.

9/6

From city, eyes cast down upon the street,
(Each person wrapped in privacy and speed,
Copper coin, slab of sky from blacktop roof) –
To country hilltop, sunrise/sunsets sweet,
(The smell of good earth, flowers; every need
Supplied past wildest dreams, beyond all proof) –
I blaze with gratitude; for subways/wheat!

9/7

When first I entered seventh heaven, it
Astonished me; that I had thus been shown
Through portals into new land through/with/in –
Those I sought fiercely to possess in sin.
Now evanescent bounty trumps the bone;
Yearning and sweetest answer blend and fit –
In the long loneliness/never alone!

8.

Poor am I, God knows, poor as withered leaf;
Poorer or richer than, I dare not ask.
To love aright, for me were hopeless task,
Eternities too high to comprehend.
But shall I tear my heart in hopeless grief,
Or rise and climb, and run and kneel, and bend,
And drink the primal love – so love in chief?

9.

Then love shall wake and be its own high life.
Then shall I know 'tis I that love indeed –
Ready, without a moment's questioning strife,
To be forgot, like bursting water-bead,
For the high good of the eternal dear;
All hope, all claim, resting, with spirit clear,
Upon the living love that every love doth breed.

10.

Ever seem to fail in utterance.
Sometimes amid the swift melodious dance
Of fluttering words – as if it had not been,
The thought has melted, vanished into night;
Sometimes I say a thing I did not mean,
And lo! 'tis better, by thy ordered chance,
Than what eluded me, floating too feathery light.

11.

If thou wouldst have me speak, Lord, give me speech.
So many cries are uttered now-a-days,
That scarce a song, however clear and true,
Will thread the jostling tumult safe, and reach
The ears of men buz-filled with poor denays:
Barb thou my words with light, make my song new,
And men will hear, or when I sing or preach.

9/8

Your mother died; my father went away.
You are a father; I am solitude.
You had and lost far more and yet can give
Even your deepest griefs to help us live;
Thus while the tomb-facts may be (Lord, God!) viewed,
Dawn of Jerusalem gives newborns food –
Milky white solace-mists at break of day.

9/9

Acceptance, altogether, of God's will;
Acceptance, taking in and praising all
The gifts, both sharp and sweet, that teach anew
How to grow evermore in his love true.
We walk in mystery, his silent call
 Summons us to the banquet on the hill,
 Out of the penitence after the fall.

9/10

Truly we are as rainbarrels to rain,
All etched by memories, patinas fine,
Sending our thirsty prayers into thy light,
Receiving each right word as rainbow sign;
You change rainwater into holy wine.
Burnishing us as we become more bright –
Seared by thy promise on the brow of Cain!

9/11

Sing, preach, and pray through us, all-knowing dear,
Even if only one small person hear
The seedling whisper in the hurricane.
The truths you give us root, and wither fear.
Dandelion pinwheels float down the lane
Of the dream; we wake and marvel to find
Fragrant primroses in our own right mind!

12.

Can anything go wrong with me? I ask –
And the same moment, at a sudden pain,
Stand trembling. Up from the great river's brim
Comes a cold breath; the farther bank is dim;
The heaven is black with clouds and coming rain;
High soaring faith is grown a heavy task,
And all is wrong with weary heart and brain.

13.

"Things do go wrong. I know grief, pain, and fear.
I see them lord it sore and wide around."
From her fair twilight answers Truth, star-crowned,
"Things wrong are needful where wrong things abound.
Things go not wrong; but Pain, with dog and spear,
False faith from human hearts will hunt and hound.
The earth shall quake 'neath them that trust the solid ground."

14.

Things go not wrong when sudden I fall prone,
But when I snatch my upheld hand from thine,
And, proud or careless, think to walk alone.
Then things go wrong, when I, poor, silly sheep,
To shelves and pits from the good pasture creep;
Not when the shepherd leaves the ninety and nine,
And to the mountains goes, after the foolish one.

15.

Lo! now thy swift dogs, over stone and bush,
After me, straying sheep, loud barking, rush.
There's *Fear*, and *Shame*, and *Empty-heart*, and *Lack*,
And *Lost-love*, and a thousand at their back!
I see thee not, but know thou hound'st them on,
And I am lost indeed – escape is none.
See! there they come, down streaming on my track!

9/12

I thought I had to pray in perfect peace,
With cheery zest and heart uplifted high.
On one day (mind a fist, defeated, fake –
The vulture of Prometheus close by)
I prayed in fury, "God! Give me a break!"
He gave me just that – wonders never cease –
And I caught blue bream in a southern lake.

9/13

In rock-a-bye-baby, the bough will break –
Baby and cradle come down from the tree.
When the wind blows, we may quake, sing or sigh,
Knowing the lullaby is for our sake.
When the pierced saviour hung apple-high, he
Reversed Newton's earth-law of gravity;
Now when the old bough breaks we rise and fly!

9/14

Go after me, Lord, should I think to stray.
I haven't time for detours anymore,
Except those you provide to teach me how
To hear thy still, small, voice, respond and pray –
Ever to be at one in thee; the core
Of all I do, of all I think and say –
With gratitude in thy eternal Now.

9/15

Death, Regret, Remorse and *Despair* track me!
This little sheep can climb no windswept tree.
Thistles and saltwort sting my matted fleece
The longer I flee thy justice and peace.
My elders were shorn, killed – I fear their fates;
A hush falls, the barking of dogs abates....
I'm lifted, loved, woven into thy *We*.

16.

I rise and run, staggering – double and run. –
But whither? – whither? – whither for escape?
The sea lies all about this long-necked cape –
There come the dogs, straight for me every one –
Me, live despair, live centre of alarms! –
Ah! lo! 'twixt me and all his barking harms,
The shepherd, lo! – I run – fall folded in his arms.

17.

There let the dogs yelp, let them growl and leap;
It is no matter – I will go to sleep.
Like a spent cloud pass pain and grief and fear,
Out from behind it unchanged love shines clear. –
Oh, save me, Christ! – I know not what I am,
I was thy stupid, self-willed, greedy lamb,
Would be thy honest and obedient sheep.

18.

Why is it that so often I return
From social converse with a spirit worn,
A lack, a disappointment – even a sting
Of shame, as for some low, unworthy thing? –
Because I have not, careful, first of all,
Set my door open wide, back to the wall,
Ere I at others' doors did knock and call.

19.

Yet more and more of me thou dost demand;
My faith and hope in God alone shall stand,
The life of law – not trust the rain and sun
To draw the golden harvest o'er the land.
I must not say – "This too will pass and die,"
"The wind will change," "Round will the seasons run."
Law is the body of will, of conscious harmony.

9/16

You pick the stickers out and gently calm
My quick heart-beat; the power of thy blood,
The blesséd solace of thy punctured palm!
High on thy shoulders, safe and found, I bleat,
My breath upon thy neck, my muddy feet
Feeling thy heart-tide infinite at flood,
Singing the rhythms of an ancient psalm.

9/17

Upon the hill of ecstasy so high
I could see heaven through its trees of oak,
Doubt tunneled under roots, a patient mole,
'Til a foggy chill enveloped my soul.
Oh, save me, Christ! In shadow time be nigh;
At sunrise, card my wool and weave my yoke,
Over and under in thy seamless cloak.

9/18

'Twas hurt that made me bolt my doors so tight,
And live in hermitage with clouds for friends,
Troubled (as when tame farm ducks start and cry
To see the wild migration *V's* stream by)
By town-talk and that spark that stirs the light
Of longing for a partner. Childhood ends,
Some of us are alone, and God knows why.

9/19

Thy will be done (I will thy will for me) –
Grafted once more into my natural tree,
I weather seasons; see each blazing leaf
That clings or flies in time's velocity.
Bright bluegray day, rain, shine – wind at gale-force,
So strong it moves the mighty clouds past grief:
I live deep in the root of thee, my source!

20.

Who trusts a law, might worship a god of wood;
Half his soul slumbers, if it be not dead.
He is a live thing shut in chaos crude,
Hemmed in with dragons – a remorseless head
Still hanging over its uplifted eyes.
No; God is all in all, and nowhere dies –
The present heart and thinking will of good.

21.

Law is our schoolmaster. Our master, Christ,
Lived under all our laws, yet always prayed –
So walked the water when the storm was highest. –
Law is Thy father's; thou hast it obeyed,
And it thereby subject to thee hast made –
To rule it, master, for thy brethren's sakes: –
Well may he guide the law by whom law's maker makes.

22.

Death haunts our souls with dissolution's strife;
Soaks them with unrest; makes our every breath
A throe, not action; from God's purest gift
Wipes off the bloom; and on the harp of faith
Its fretted strings doth slacken still and shift:
Life everywhere, perfect, and always life,
Is sole redemption from this haunting death.

23.

God, thou from death dost lift me. As I rise,
Its Lethe from my garment drips and flows.
Ere long I shall be safe in upper air,
With thee, my life – with thee, my answered prayer
Where thou art God in every wind that blows,
And self alone, and ever, softly dies,
There shall my being blossom, and I know it fair.

9/20

A living God within us, infinite;
A living faith that breathes as we are breathed,
Forgiven, conscience seeds and yields new bloom,
Else church is just a decorated room,
Rote prayers a donkey's tail to pin in it.
The sun's an apricot this morn, bequeathed
To us in lilac sky upon God's loom!

9/21

When trusted servants use dead law to rule,
Condemning sinners with self-righteous shout –
Great wisdom flows in radiance from a fool;
A child turns expectations inside out,
Catching the Pharisees in their own net.
The risen Christ eats fish, forgives our debt –
We walk in faith upon a lake of doubt.

9/22

I love the number ~22~ like swans
Who mate for life they glide in tranquil twain
On lake, at sea, in sunlight and in rain;
At tomb's edge I'm at once belovéd (John's
Gift) and bereft as weeping Magdalene –
The folded headcloth and the angels bright:
Swan gone, and Swan Beyond in living light!

9/23

Those who had dim mirage for self must first
Stop being who each circumstance requires,
And receive, learn to bear the "I" (best/worst),
Burn the chameleon in eternal fires,
Begin to be the nascent child of thirst
And hunger being shaped upon thy wheel;
Then wed thee, smash self-vessel, become real!

24.

I would dig, Master, in no field but thine,
Would build my house only upon thy rock,
Yet am but a dull day, with a sea-sheen!
Why should I wonder then that they should mock,
Who, in the limbo of things heard and seen,
Hither and thither blowing, lose the shine
Of every light that hangs in the firmament divine.

25.

Lord, loosen in me the hold of visible things;
Help me to walk by faith and not by sight;
I would, through thickest veils and coverings,
See into the chambers of the living light.
Lord, in the land of things that swell and seem,
Help me to walk by the other light supreme,
Which shows thy facts behind man's vaguely hinting dream.

26.

I see a little child whose eager hands
Search the thick stream that drains the crowded street
For possible things hid in its current slow.
Near by, behind him, a great palace stands,
Where kings might welcome nobles to their feet.
Soft sounds, sweet scents, fair sights there only go –
There the child's father lives, but the child does not know.

27.

On, eager, hungry, busy-seeking child,
Rise up, turn round, run in, run up the stair.
Far in a chamber from rude noise exiled,
Thy father sits, pondering how thou dost fare.
The mighty man will clasp thee to his breast:
Will kiss thee, stroke the tangles of thy hair,
And lap thee warm in fold on fold of lovely rest.

9/24

Polished like hard stones by the seaside tide,
Ground to fine sand (in hour-glass/on beach) –
You are the mortar, Lord. I sculpt in time my
Chapel-home, all the while buffeted by
Illusions of security. Make each
Mirror a window, Architect; abide
Within us, star so far beyond our reach!

9/25

Lord, when I marvel at the world I see,
Give me a painter's eye (no wordly goal
To get between thy mystery and me).
As icons be the windows to thy day,
White yogurt-trails in empty, dark-blue bowl
Invite me to traverse the Milky Way –
And make a map for heart, mind, hope and soul!

9/26

In the dense city, the dog walks me (she
And I sniffing along the sidewalk for
Scents and sequins, lost barettes; both of us
Short-leashed, imprisoned) beside the tour bus.
Only by climbing five steep flights may we
Open the secretly unlatched roof-door,
Look up and see in clouds Almighty More.

9/27

I can't imagine solace such as this;
Cannot imagine trusting such embrace.
If you can untangle my hair, Lord, you
Can surely dismantle my fear of bliss.
What I can't imagine, I still may face –
Even believe – impossible and new;
Tenderest love sprung from bitterest rue.

28.

The prince of this world came, and nothing found
In thee, O master; but, ah, woe is me!
He cannot pass me, on other business bound,
But, spying in me things familiar, he
Casts over me the shadow of his flight,
And straight I moan in darkness – and the fight
Begins afresh betwixt the world and thee.

29.

In my own heart, O master, in my thought,
Betwixt the woolly sheep and hairy goat
Not clearly I distinguish; but I think
Thou knowest that I fight upon thy side.
The *how* I am ashamed of; for I shrink
From many a blow – am borne on the battle-tide,
When I should rush to the front, and take thy foe by the
throat.

30.

The enemy still hath many things in me;
Yea, many an evil nest with open hole
Gapes out to him, at which he enters free.
But, like the impact of a burning coal,
His presence mere straight rouses the garrison,
And all are up in arms, and down on knee,
Fighting and praying till the foe is gone.

9/28

Many things wrong today (not over yet):
To buy something for a house I don't own,
I locked myself out of the one I'm in;
After the locksmith (and self-damning din),
Backed into a car by a pumpkin bin;
All I see now is my own shameful debt,
And I feel for the moment quite alone.

9/29

I've bred some hybrids in my mind: a *geep*
Has horns to menace foes, unlike a sheep;
A *shoat* can gently "baaa", thus confound wraths.
When it comes time to choose between two paths -
Between the hanging thieves, there is one choice:
High road or low road, shepherd, let me keep
Listening, that I may obey your voice.

9/30

I am the swept room – seven demons sow
Here: gluttony, lust, envy, avarice,
Plus three. I started late. With each strong play
I see how very far I have to go
To banish my tenacious, dug-in foe.
On my knees in despair at the abyss,
I feel my small good rise like bread of day.

OCTOBER.

1.

REMEMBER, Lord, thou hast not made me good.
Or if thou didst, it was so long ago
I have forgotten – and never understood,
I humbly think. At best it was a crude,
A rough-hewn goodness, that did need this woe,
This sin, these harms of all kinds fierce and rude,
To shape it out, making it live and grow.

2.

But thou art making me, I thank thee, sire.
What thou hast done and doest thou know'st well,
And I will help thee: – gently in thy fire
I will lie burning; on thy potter's-wheel
I will whirl patient, though my brain should reel;
Thy grace shall be enough the grief to quell,
And growing strength perfect through weakness dire.

3.

I have not knowledge, wisdom, insight, thought,
Nor understanding, fit to justify
Thee in thy work, O Perfect. Thou hast brought
Me up to this – and, lo! what thou hast wrought,
I cannot call it good. But I can cry –
"O enemy, the maker hath not done;
One day thou shalt behold, and from the sight wilt run."

OCTOBER

10/1

Perhaps I love old things because their scars,
(The visible patinas of *withstand*,
Endure) encourage me as apple-bloom
Fades. Others have looked at the perfect stars
And marvelled, on their hearts a cross+hatched hand.
Weave thou our wonder on thy divine loom,
And when our thread snaps, free us from the tomb!

10/2

Can grace quell grief? Perhaps this grief *is* grace.
Turning within thy hands we glimpse thy face
And rise up slippery with anguished tears;
Baked in thy kiln, O Potter, with our fears'
Remembered textures. Centered we come forth –
Cooling within winds south, west, east and north –
Transformed into new form, new time, new place.

10/3

Here as rainbow frost-shards melt in the sun,
Although I breakfast on green apples/cheese,
The fear of death rides on each falling leaf,
And I am landlocked in premature grief.
I cannot scare the enemy, but please –
Since he is strong and I am on my knees –
Take me with wild geese on their freedom run!

4.

The faith I will, aside is easily bent;
But of thy love, my God, one glimpse alone
Can make me absolutely confident –
With faith, hope, joy, in love responsive blent.
My soul then, in the vision mighty grown,
Its father and its fate securely known,
Falls on thy bosom with exultant moan.

5.

Thou workest perfectly. And if it seem
Some things are not so well, 'tis but because
They are too loving-deep, too lofty-wise,
For me, poor child, to understand their laws:
My highest wisdom half is but a dream;
My love runs helpless like a falling stream:
Thy good embraces ill, and lo! its illness dies!

6.

From sleep I wake, and wake to think of thee.
But wherefore not with sudden glorious glee?
Why burst not gracious on me heaven and earth
In all the splendour of a new-day-birth?
Why hangs a cloud betwixt my lord and me?
The moment that my eyes the morning greet,
My soul should panting rush to clasp thy father-feet.

7.

Is it because it is not thou I see,
But only my poor, blotted fancy of thee?
Oh! never till thyself reveal thy face,
Shall I be flooded with life's vital grace.
Oh make my mirror-heart thy shining-place,
And then my soul, awaking with the morn,
Shall be a waking joy, eternally new-born.

10/4

Cello on the radio; rain outside,
In a fallen country, in failing health –
The cat throws up, the dog patiently waits –
I strive for breath. We cannot know our fates.
Within this casque of sorrow, thy great wealth
Of love intact lets me know you abide,
And will win through once this despair has died.

10/5

The mighty clouds pass over, vast and high
Above small worries and whirlpooling care.
Lord, will we destroy your creation now?
Thy peace is not a plateau prayers buy;
I breathe in and out this bright autumn air,
Having no wisdom. We cannot know how
You will save us from our folly, nor why.

10/6

All I should do hangs overhead each morn'.
I wake from dreams to failure; each small task
Confirms my imperfection. Such self-scorn
Obstructs the prayer intention (I'm too bad!) –
Yet I pray: "Lord, take away this death mask."
Sunrise: with each new breath I am new-born.
Cold pink petunias stand in light – brave/glad.

10/7

When on all fours beside the road (the dog
Licks my face saying: *live!*), you are the word
Help! without the breath to say it. As sure
Of death as I was, no image came; fog
Closing in, dark, body failing, I heard
Nothing, just caught a tiny breath, as pure
As hope itself; so I came to your lure.

8.

Lord, in my silver is much metal base,
Else should my being by this time have shown
Thee thy own self therein. Therefore do I
Wake in the furnace. I know thou sittest by,
Refining – look, keep looking in to try
Thy silver; master, look and see thy face,
Else here I lie for ever, blank as any stone.

9.

But when in the dim silver thou dost look,
I do behold thy face, though blurred and faint.
Oh joy! no flaw in me thy grace will brook,
But still refine: slow shall the silver pass
From bright to brighter, till, sans spot or taint,
Love, well content, shall see no speck of brass,
And I his perfect face shall hold as in a glass.

10.

With every morn my life afresh must break
The crust of self, gathered about me fresh;
That thy wind-spirit may rush in and shake
The darkness out of me, and rend the mesh
The spider-devils spin out of the flesh –
Eager to net the soul before it wake,
That it may slumberous lie, and listen to the snake.

11.

'Tis that I am not good – that is enough;
I pry no farther – that is not the way.
Here, O my potter, is thy making stuff!
Set thy wheel going; let it whir and play.
The chips in me, the stones, the straws, the sand,
Cast them out with fine separating hand,
And make a vessel of thy yielding clay.

10/8

I can't aspire to silver; clay and stone
Are marvels; a bead of blue glass in earth
Discovered seems to me gem of great worth.
I would be a seashell in thy pierced palm,
A fragment of Eve's reliquary bone.
Oil me with chrism, sweat, blood, tears, new birth –
Do touch me, now and then – be thou my balm.

10/9

Within thy silvered mirror all-benign,
Like a miniature of thy design,
I lie in thy palm's grace at the life line,
(Cut so short to beget our Beulah Land).
So within me a tiny grain of sand
That once was mighty cliff begins (a girl)
The journey to become (perhaps) a pearl.

10/10

Tethered to world-speak and medicines new,
Looking at homestead with vagabond eyes,
Wounded in subtle nets; too slow by far,
Like the five wood-beetles caught in small jar;
Captive at daybreak, Lord – break through mute cries.
Purpose and peace, please; I can't eat the view!
Where is the narrow way, found by thy few?

10/11

Make of me a chalice, a loving cup,
When I fall, center me and draw me up;
When I am wobbly, do thou pull me in,
Far from the tempting glazes of my sin;
Help me to see you in my neighbor's face.
Of common clay, I rise and (conscious) spin
Toward Potter's Field, my final resting place.

12.

What if it take a thousand years to make me,
So me he leave not, angry, on the floor! –
Nay, thou art never angry! – that would break me!
Would I tried never thy dear patience sore,
But were as good as thou couldst well expect me,
Whilst thou dost make, I mar, and thou correct me!
Then were I now content, waiting for something more.

13.

Only, my God, see thou that I content thee –
Oh, take thy own content upon me, God!
Ah, never, never, sure, wilt thou repent thee,
That thou hast called thy Adam from the clod!
Yet must I mourn that thou shouldst ever find me
One moment sluggish, needing more of the rod
Than thou didst think when thy desire designed me.

14.

My God, it troubles me I am not better.
More help, I pray, still more. Thy perfect debtor
I shall be when thy perfect child I am grown.
My Father, help me – am I not thine own?
Lo, other lords have had dominion o'er me,
But now thy will alone I set before me:
Thy own heart's life – Lord, thou wilt not abhor me!

15.

In youth, when once again I had set out
To find thee, Lord, my life, my liberty,
A window now and then, clouds all about,
Would open into heaven: my heart forlorn
First all would tremble with a solemn glee,
Then, whelmed in peace, rest like a man outworn,
That sees the dawn slow part the closed lids of the morn.

10/12

This black sheep, knitting hats from her own wool,
Shorn, chilly, (and likely to unravel
The mental construct that keeps her ears warm)
Prays in confusion: *Lord's will, fill me full
Of surrender.* Sheep don't rule, nor travel
Far from their shepherd, deep into the storm –
I have the text, Lord: let me live the form.

10/13

What my purpose is I do not know, though
Over and over I beg you to show
Where it is (past youth) you wish me to go,
What my right work is, how I am to live.
Shall I publish a want ad? "Although blessed
To be right here-and-now in time, caressed
By this sweet breeze – solo Eve longs to give."

10/14

The translators who split on "trespass/debt"
Gave consciousness of testaments old/new,
Things concrete/immaterial, law/love,
Justice/mercy, slingshot/dowserwand. Let
Me submit all such divisions to you.
Transform my hawk-DNA into dove,
And free me from this self, the fowler's net.

10/15

On carousel, I set out for brass ring,
(Not knowing there was such a thing as gold),
Well versed, closed-circle, no-god, dead-end spin.
Years later, dizzy, been-there-done-that – in
Despair, fell through centrifugal stronghold,
Upon my knees and there began to sing:
Help me, dear Jesus! I'll do anything!

16.

Now I grow old, and the soft-gathered years
Have calmed, yea dulled the heart's swift fluttering beat;
But a quiet hope that keeps its household seat
Is better than recurrent glories fleet.
To know thee, Lord, is worth a many tears;
And when this mildew, age, has dried away,
My heart will beat again as young and strong and gay.

17.

Stronger and gayer tenfold! – but, O friends,
Not for itself, nor any hoarded bliss.
I see but vaguely whither my being tends,
All vaguely spy a glory shadow-blent,
Vaguely desire the "individual kiss;"
But when I think of God, a large content
Fills the dull air of my gray cloudy tent.

18.

Father of me, thou art my bliss secure.
Make of me, maker, whatsoe'er thou wilt.
Let fancy's wings hang moulting, hope grow poor,
And doubt steam up from where a joy was spilt –
I lose no time to reason it plain and clear,
But fly to thee, my life's perfection dear: –
Not what I think, but what thou art, makes sure.

19.

This utterance of spirit through still thought,
This forming of heart-stuff in moulds of brain,
Is helpful to the soul by which 'tis wrought,
The shape reacting on the heart again;
But when I am quite old, and words are slow,
Like dying things that keep their holes for woe,
And memory's withering tendrils clasp with effort vain?

10/16

Now I grow old, never quite having bloomed;
Like this maple branch, broken off in wind –
Half attached, as cold air chills the sap. Still
I love those I gave my heart to; consumed,
As soon this branch will be, by flame. Who sinned
Will be invited to thy banquet; fill
Me with gratitude, here, *over the hill.*

10/17

This morning I saw sunrise – holy gift!
All my years in the city I did not.
It rose so red, then turned into white gold!
Rise in my being; loosen the hard knot
Of what-ifs and what-nexts. I cannot drift
Into imagined Glory – I am cold.
Why do I feel so young and am so old?

10/18

I cannot reason – labyrinth my mind.
I hold to thee as tiny child must hold
The loop in jump-rope when the light turns green.
Am I going or coming? Make me kind,
(Though I forever feel betwixt/between)
Lead me by thinnest thread as I unwind,
Spun like a foretold top into thy fold.

10/19

I cannot plan ahead; *now* is too hard.
Brain cookies baked today in future will
Be broken, eaten, shared when road is dire –
Or given to the birds. Thanks be! You still
Have taken care to touch me and to fill
My cracked-cup heart with love; to light each shard
With the bright blue flame of the Holy Fire.

20.

Thou, then as now, no less wilt be my life,
And I shall know it better than before,
Praying and trusting, hoping, claiming more.
From effort vain, sick foil, and bootless strife,
I shall, with childness fresh, look up to thee;
Thou, seeing thy child with age encumbered sore,
Wilt round him bend thine arm more carefully.

21.

And when grim Death doth take me by the throat,
Thou wilt have pity on thy handiwork;
Thou wilt not let him on my suffering gloat,
But draw my soul out – gladder than man or boy,
When thy saved creatures from the narrow ark
Rushed out, and leaped and laughed and cried for joy,
And the great rainbow strode across the dark.

22.

Against my fears, my doubts, my ignorance,
I trust in thee, O father of my Lord!
The world went on in this same broken dance,
When, worn and mocked, he trusted and adored:
I too will trust, and gather my poor best
To face the truth-faced false. So in his nest
I shall awake at length, a little scarred and scored.

23.

Things cannot look all right so long as I
Am not all right who see – therefore not right
Can see. The lamp within sends out the light
Which shows the things; and if its rays go wry,
Or are not white, they must part show a lie.
The man, half-cured, did men not trees conclude,
Because he moving saw what else had seemed a wood.

10/20

O! for a faith like this – that as leaves fall,
Belief persists, grows stronger. You live here
Within/around me, you help me to bear
Unknowing, loss, grim failure, ghostly fear,
Help me to know you near when I feel small;
Uphold me when I cannot see through care –
Walking life/death tightrope in autumn's hall.

10/21

Let Death and Judas be my midwives when
I leave my shell behind and reach the tolls
Where both accused/defended I shall be.
Let (somewhere on a farm or on the sea)
Someone say one strong prayer to shelter me.
May I be fit to stand among good souls,
Or hatch in fire, Jerusalem God-hen!

10/22

Riding the sacred Name, a leaf in flood –
(Each vein a rib of ark, I drown and float;
The benediction of the rainbow sign
Miraculous above a world of mud) –
Here in thy deep, beyond earth-nets, lifeboat,
Dove Holy Spirit and her branch-in-bud
Leads to the new dawn in thy day divine.

10/23

We cannot quite discern man from his tree.
It is right lonely at the cross/fireplace –
Noting a pattern in the glowing wood
Which falls to ash before another see.
Strip false illusions from my sight; let good
Clear vision light both wonderful and base.
Set thy flame in my heart – illumine me!

24.

Give me, take from me, as thou wilt. I learn –
Slowly and stubbornly I learn to yield
With a strange hopefulness. As from the field
Of hard-fought battle won, the victor chief
Turns thankfully, although his heart do yearn,
So from my old things to thy new I turn,
With sad, thee-trusting heart, and not in grief.

25.

If with my father I did wander free,
Floating o'er hill and field where'er we would,
And, lighting on the sward before the door,
Strange faces through the window-panes should see,
And strange feet standing where the loved had stood,
The dear old place theirs all, as ours before –
Should I be sorrowful, father, having thee?

26.

So, Lord, if thou tak'st from me all the rest,
Thyself with each resumption drawing nigher,
It shall but hurt me as the thorn of the briar,
When I reach to the pale flower in its breast.
To have thee, Lord, is to have all thy best,
Holding it by its very life divine –
To let my friend's hand go, and take his heart in mine.

27.

Take from me leisure, all familiar places;
Take all the lovely things of earth and air
Take from me books; take all my precious faces;
Take words melodious, and their songful linking;
Take scents, and sounds, and all thy outsides fair;
Draw nearer, taking, and, to my sober thinking,
Thou bring'st them nearer all, and ready to my prayer.

10/24

I used to leap from unacknowledged want
Direct to renunciation, without
Knowing/imagining the *having* joy.
Now in the tides of thy baptismal font,
Receiving/leaving, certain or in doubt –
I seek thy will. Though I am dim alloy,
May each small leading make me more devout.

10/25

Once ever I had loved, I found it hard
And sorrowful to lose the other half.
I always, ever after, felt the loss
As though my grief had turned to graveyard moss
Upon stone-proof of love. I take my staff,
And walk on (lonely) through the scent of nard,
But when I thank you, Father, I shall laugh.

10/26

Just so, in icons of the Sacred Heart,
A thorn circlet may pierce the shining rays,
And pentecostal flame enshrine thy cross.
I only know each thing I want brings loss;
I live in answered prayers by thy art,
Though I can't own the love/my friend/our days;
I'll be good loser – learn to play that part.

10/27

So versed in letting go I can't hold on,
Prepared for lack's eventuality,
Defective in this, that, and the other:
Belief, right action, real love of brother.
This rainy day obeisance falls upon
A variation of "Don't leave me, John!" –
Namely, "Lord God, please don't give up on me!"

28.

No place on earth henceforth I shall count strange,
For every place belongeth to my Christ.
I will go calm where'er thou bid'st me range;
Whoe'er my neighbour, thou art still my nighest.
Oh my heart's life, my owner, will of my being!
Into my soul thou every moment diest,
In thee my life thus evermore decreeing.

29.

What though things change and pass, nor come again!
Thou, the life-heart of all things, changest never.
The sun shines on; the fair clouds turn to rain,
And glad the earth with many a spring and river.
The hearts that answer change with chill and shiver,
That mourn the past, sad-sick, with hopeless pain,
They know not thee, our changeless heart and brain.

30.

My halting words will some day turn to song –
Some far-off day, in holy other times!
The melody now prisoned in my rimes
Will one day break aloft, and from the throng
Of wrestling thoughts and words spring up the air;
As from the flower its colour's sweet despair
Issues in odour, and the sky's low levels climbs.

31.

My surgent thought shoots lark-like up to thee.
Thou like the heaven art all about the lark.
Whatever I surmise or know in me,
Idea, or but symbol on the dark,
Is living, working, thought-creating power
In thee, the timeless father of the hour.
I am thy book, thy song – thy child would be.

10/28

The birthmark on my forehead is a *V,*
Twenty-two in the alphabet, a sign,
Five, Capricorn, antennae, victory.
You die/we praise in every *Y* of tree.
In U division ends: Cain's mark – divine
Assurance/stain upon the chastened brow –
Symbol of longing in the here and now.

10/29

Imperturbable constancy, anchor
Beyond creation, heart of lovingkind –
Keep us past time and space within thy peace,
Harmony, forgiveness, vanished rancor;
Afloat in homing forcefield without cease,
Within sheep's cloud, star spiraling heaven's mind –
And when, full-shorn, I bleat, bless thou my fleece!

10/30

World wildfires rage as green-pink primrose bed,
Wild roses and chrysanthemums as well
Bespeak a tranquil grace (advent trumps law).
October takes her mournful leave, crows caw.
In Mary's seventh month, *Emmanuel*
Stirs in the temple as she bakes the bread,
Humming so sweetly she consoles the dead.

10/31

I take a wasp outside, am stupor-blissed.
I see a hummingbird on wire high,
And add another task to my long list:
"Feed birds, show lady bug the door, brush teeth".
Snap-dragons in white window-boxes die.
How is it that you bless and so bequeath
Perfection (as this day) to such as I?

NOVEMBER

1.

THOU art of this world, Christ. Thou know'st it all;
Thou know'st our evens, our morns, our red and gray;
How moons, and hearts, and seasons rise and fall;
How we grow weary plodding on the way;
Of future joy how present pain bereaves,
Rounding us with a dark of mere decay,
Tossed with a drift of summer-fallen leaves.

2.

Thou knowest all our weeping, fainting, striving;
Thou know'st how very hard it is *to be*;
How hard to rouse faint will not yet reviving;
To do the pure thing, trusting all to thee;
To hold thou art there, for all no face we see;
How hard to think, through cold and dark and dearth,
That thou art nearer now than when eye-seen on earth.

3.

Have pity on us for the look of things,
When blank denial stares us in the face.
Although the serpent mask have lied before,
It fascinates the bird that darkling sings,
And numbs the little prayer-bird's beating wings.
For how believe thee somewhere in blank space,
If through the darkness come no knocking to our door?

NOVEMBER

11/1

I feel thy beauty in the present tense,
Within the pain and through it, recompense
Enough. As moments of this life sweep by,
Am I to seek redemption in the sky?
All leaves have blown down from my tree of sense;
The future joy I cannot yet forsee -
As my illusions die, Lord, be with me!

11/2

Why bloody warfare, far as eye can see?
Is Barabbas as strong as he appears?
Folk songs as old as Mary's lullaby,
An empty nest high in a naked tree,
Artesian welling stream of ceaseless tears.
Farewell, love of my heart of hearts, goodbye:
Hello, rain – Sunday, Blessed Trinity!

11/3

O Giver, naked, hung between two thieves,
Barabbas drinking to your endless death –
"Your eye is on me" – this each bird believes
Though mesmerized by charismatic priest.
You know 'twixt hope and hell we sparrows feast
Or starve, fly/fall within thy holy breath.
There are no doors but grace in church of Beth.

4.

If we might sit until the darkness go,
Possess our souls in patience perhaps we might;
But there is always something to be done,
And no heart left to do it. To and fro
The dull thought surges, as the driven waves fight
In gulfy channels. Oh! victorious one,
Give strength to rise, go out, and meet thee in the night.

5.

"Wake, thou that sleepest; rise up from the dead,
And Christ will give thee light." I do not know
What sleep is, what is death, or what is light;
But I am waked enough to feel a woe,
To rise and leave death. Stumbling through the night,
To my dim lattice, O calling Christ! I go,
And out into the dark look for thy star-crowned head.

6.

There are who come to me, and write, and send,
Whom I would love, giving good things to all,
But *friend* – that name I cannot on them spend;
'Tis from the centre of self-love they call
For cherishing – for which they first must know
How to be still, and take the seat that's low:
When, Lord, shall I be fit – when wilt thou call me friend?

7.

Wilt thou not one day, Lord? In all my wrong,
Self-love and weakness, laziness and fear,
This one thing I can say: *I am content*
To be and have what in thy heart I am meant
To be and have. In my best times I long
After thy will, and think it glorious-dear;
Even in my worst, perforce my will to thine is bent.

11/4

My father left home in the "last" World War.
Give strength to move toward one, beyond the door,
Who incarnates true reciprocity –
That baby steps, in time, may lead to thee.
Call me as though the purpose of my birth
Is clear somewhere, and dawn deep within me
As sun auroras stream to autumn earth.

11/5

Why should I shelter under tin-can roof
When solar winds and iridescent mists
Sweep through thy stars and cause small dogs to bark?
I would swap fear for wonder. Sages' lists
Assure me you are present in this dark
To teach me love without a daylight proof.
Through gravecloth, I sing wobbly praise – O, hark!

11/6

I have few friends, so know not how to be
A friend to man or beast or Master great.
I am too small and star-struck. Do I just
Exit my prison, enter heaven's gate?
Who called me friend betrayed me. Shall I trust
Time to perfect me? I need grace to see
(Since I know nothing) you are Friend to me.

11/7

I realize that I can kill a fly.
Chilled in self-hatred, swamped by human flaws
And major sins, a failure it must seem;
Still, I may pray to live within the dream
In which I do no wrong, and follow thy
Will, hoping you give me leave just here to pause:
And skip my jump-rope in the dragon's jaws.

8.

My God, I look to thee for tenderness
Such as I could not seek from any man,
Or in a human heart fancy or plan –
A something deepest prayer will not express:
Lord, with thy breath blow on my being's fires,
Until, even to the soul with self-love wan,
I yield the primal love, that no return desires.

9.

Only no word of mine must ever foster
The self that in a brother's bosom gnaws;
I may not fondle failing, nor the boaster
Encourage with the breath of my applause.
Weakness needs pity, sometimes love's rebuke;
Strength only sympathy deserves and draws –
And grows by every faithful loving look.

10.

'Tis but as men draw nigh to thee, my Lord,
They can draw nigh each other and not hurt.
Who with the gospel of thy peace are girt,
The belt from which doth hang the Spirit's sword,
Shall breathe on dead bones, and the bones shall live,
Sweet poison to the evil self shall give,
And, clean themselves, lift men clean from the mire abhorred.

11.

My Lord, I have no clothes to come to thee;
My shoes are pierced and broken with the road;
I am torn and weathered, wounded with the goad,
And soiled with tugging at my weary load:
The more I need thee! A very prodigal
I stagger into thy presence, Lord of me:
One look, my Christ, and at thy feet I fall!

11/8

The Little Mermaid, pearly, deep in sea –
Was my high standard when my heart was wild
With unrequited, needy jealousy.
'Till I *come round right*, Father, help me turn.
As you have loved me (with such dim return),
Help me to learn to love unselfishly,
That I may truly come to be thy child.

11/9

Feed on you in our hearts with thanksgiving,
Say Episcopalians at our low rail.
Through, with, in you, in the unity of
The Holy Spirit, we Catholics, living
In twain with Orthodox – all taste in love
Fountain of Immortality: name, nail
And thorn-crown thee, Lord, King of Jews above!

11/10

Fear turns to anger, and the belt of peace
Around the globe is rent by bombs of war
(Called *bombs of peace* by men who drop these bombs).
The clergy worldwide conjures up the psalms
Which served to strengthen all pure souls of yore,
And make strong mead for those who now release
The rage that taints our praying-without-cease.

11/11

Ah, leave me not outside in exile's lair
Because I've not right clothes and am not yet
All you would have me be! Past contempt's glare,
I make my way, bowed down with profound debt,
To venerate with tears, and dry with hair,
The source of my forgivenness unearned.
Give me the loving heart for which I've yearned!

12.

Why should I still hang back, like one in a dream,
Who vainly strives to clothe himself aright,
That in great presence he may seemly seem?
Why call up feeling? – dress me in the faint,
Worn, faded, cast-off nimbus of some saint?
Why of old mood bring back a ghostly gleam –
While there He waits, love's heart and loss's blight!

13.

Son of the Father, elder brother mine,
See thy poor brother's plight; See how he stands
Defiled and feeble, hanging down his hands!
Make me clean, brother, with thy burning shine;
From thy rich treasures, householder divine,
Bring forth fair garments, old and new, I pray,
And like thy brother dress me, in the old home-bred way.

14.

My prayer-bird was cold – would not away,
Although I set it on the edge of the nest.
Then I bethought me of the story old –
Love-fact or loving fable, thou know'st best –
How, when the children had made sparrows of clay,
Thou mad'st them birds, with wings to flutter and fold:
Take, Lord, my prayer in thy hand, and make it pray.

15.

My poor clay-sparrow seems turned to a stone,
And from my heart will neither fly nor run.
I cannot feel as thou and I both would,
But, Father, I am willing – make me good.
What art thou father for, but to help thy son?
Look deep, yet deeper, in my heart, and there,
Beyond where I can feel, read thou the prayer.

11/12

In this new Eden, children need no clothes,
No dogma-pieties; just as we are,
Immediacy of eternal now,
Within thy mercy-heart of Love we bow,
Far from the prickling envies of our foes,
We may bloom fragrant as an autumn rose,
And incandescent as a winter star.

11/13

Elder brother, son of Our Father-God,
Encourage me, that inside-out I bear
The hope that I too, possibly, will wear
Homespun fresh garments like your mother's own,
When some day I will be more holy grown.
I, work-in-progess, wash my motley odd,
And dance my grateful praises in bright air.

11/14

Did my earth-parents love each other in
The moment this clay bird began to be?
How long did dark earth-egg protect/contain
With precious lies my stunted, stubborn sin?
At last i cracked (shell, thought, sight, heart and brain)
Under the brooding mercy-breath set free:
Bough broke, nest fell, and I flew home to thee!

11/15

Beyond all feeling, Lord, Emmanuel –
Deep in the spiral of the ocean shell
Where tides unceasingly call upon thee –
Song of the *shofar*, in salt-sea water –
Create me clean, make good your new daughter.
May my dead live, forgiving me,
Until the new Jerusalem we see.

16.

Oh what it were to be right sure of thee!
Sure that thou art, and the same as thy son, Jesus!
Oh, faith is deeper, wider than the sea,
Yea, than the blue of heaven that ever flees us!
Yet simple as the cry of sore-hurt child,
Or as his shout, with sudden gladness wild,
When home from school he runs, till morn set free.

17.

If I were sure thou, Father, verily art,
True father of the Nazarene as true,
Sure as I am of my wife's shielding heart,
Sure as of sunrise in the watching blue,
Sure as I am that I do eat and drink,
And have a heart to love and laugh and think,
Meseems in flame the joy might from my body start.

18.

But I must know thee in a deeper way
Than any of these ways, or know thee not;
My heart at peace far loftier proof must lay
Than if the wind thou me the wave didst roll,
Than if I lay before thee a sunny spot,
Or knew thee as the body knows its soul,
Or even as the part doth know its perfect whole.

19.

There is no word to tell how I must know thee;
No wind clasped ever a low meadow-flower
So close that as to nearness it could show thee;
No rainbow so makes one the sun and shower.
A something with thee, I am a nothing fro' thee.
Because I am not save as I am in thee,
My soul is ever setting out to win thee.

11/16

I believe (past knowing) that you are *One*
In essence, undivided – spirit, son,
Father. Distinct is Adam from the new
Infant who (born in fragrant straw and blessed)
Is infinitely loved at Mary's breast,
First-fruit on Josephwood-cross as a Jew;
Feast, lintel lamb-blood – manna for we few.

11/17

I am the little lamb who *once was lost.*
I seek no certainty; my Pentecost
(Forgiven sinner bliss) is beeswax flame
In humbled heart, unsure, incense of praise.
Candle-wings melt as votive hopes now raise
Prayers of love unto the Lord of Days.
I have no other hearth but Jesus' name.

11/18

God's peace, thanksgivings in my heart hard by
Emotional turmoils, world-shaking wars.
While spinning plates on high-wire in strong wind,
Clown needs a balance staff but finds two oars!
The fools-cap jingles. Do you laugh at my
Awkward steps into your calm breath so high
Above the circus where I threshed and sinned?

11/19

I float within my eggshell earth-seed mound.
Here I seek to protect my kernel hope.
Without and through my cracks your strong wind blows;
Whether I hide or seek now, *lost is found.*
Surrender paved the way; the wisest pope
Might bless and chant my baby steps around –
But where I go, only the dear Lord knows.

20.

I know not how – for that I first must know thee.
I know I know thee not as I would know thee,
For my heart burns like theirs that did not know him,
Till he broke bread, and therein they must know him.
I know thee, knowing that I do not know thee,
Nor ever shall till one with me I know thee –
Even as thy son, the eternal man, doth know thee.

21.

Creation under me, in, and above,
Slopes upward from the base, a pyramid,
On whose point I shall stand at last, and love.
From the first rush of vapour at thy will,
To the last poet-word that darkness chid,
Thou hast been sending up creation's hill,
To lift thy souls aloft in faithful Godhead free.

22.

I think my thought, and fancy I think thee. –
Lord, wake me up; rend swift my coffin-planks;
I pray thee, let me live – alive and free.
My soul will break forth in melodious thanks,
Aware at last what thou wouldst have it be,
When thy life shall be light in me, and when
My life to thine is answer and amen.

23.

How oft I say the same things in these lines!
Even as a man, buried in during dark,
Turns ever where the edge of twilight shines,
Prays ever towards the vague eternal mark;
Or as the sleeper, having dreamed he drinks,
Back straightway into thirstful dreaming sinks,
So turns my will to thee, for thee still longs, still pines.

11/20

Seeking in hope that hope sustain unknowing,
Hymning the sky while fierce rainstorms are blowing,
Calling Christ "brother" strongly, with a plea –
That through-with-in-him I may mystically
Become true sister, walk in good ongoing,
As broken daughter, dough raised, baked 'till brown –
Formed in the fire-thorn circlet of his crown!

11/21

A seashell spiral blooms above the pale,
Far from mind-prison where snake eats its tail.
Some days I *turn* within the Shaker song,
Climb seven "*I Am's*", now rejoice, now grieve –
From mountaintop and belly of the whale,
Eyes closed, praying to *come round right*; the long
Road brightens – rising, we converge, believe!

11/22

Even when goodness is obscured by mist,
Shortcomings nail-sharp: hear this child who prays
To emerge one day from this forlorn haze,
And to be reawakened – ribcage raise,
Knowing each breath I take is heaven's gift.
Lord, should I wake alone, take graveyard shift,
And save me by the bell tied to my wrist.

11/23

As stars shine brightest in the sky of black,
And seedlings promise orchards in the core,
Our prayers ascend like music from the soup
Of myths, sweet lullabyes, barbaric war.
Lift and sustain our hope, forevermore,
Lord – save your earnest, motley little troupe,
Down here so far below your zodiac.

24.

The mortal man, all careful, wise, and troubled,
The eternal child in the nursery doth keep.
To-morrow on to-day the man heaps doubled;
The child laughs, hopeful, even in his sleep.
The man rebukes the child for foolish trust;
The child replies, "Thy care is for poor dust;
Be still, and let me wake that thou mayst sleep."

25.

Till I am one, with oneness manifold,
I must breed contradiction, strife, and doubt;
Things tread Thy court – look real – take proving hold –
My Christ is not yet grown to cast them out;
Alas! to me, false-judging 'twixt the twain,
The *Unseen* oft fancy seems, while, all about,
The *Seen* doth lord it with a mighty train.

26.

But when the Will hath learned obedience royal,
He straight will set the child upon the throne;
To whom the seen things all, grown instant loyal,
Will gather to his feet, in homage prone –
The child their master they have ever known;
Then shall the visible fabric plainly lean
On a Reality that never can be seen.

27.

Thy ways are wonderful, maker of men!
Thou gavest me a child, and I have fed
And clothed and loved her, many a growing year;
Lo! now a friend of months draws gently near,
And claims her future – all beyond his ken –
There he hath never loved her nor hath led:
She weeps and moans, but turns, and leaves her home so dear.

11/24

The mortal woman sleeps and will not wake;
The child works in play clothes and tries to keep
The checkbook straight, and every night she'll take
Far too much ice-cream in an antique spoon –
Then go outside and give thanks for the moon!
And when night falls and she has gone to sleep,
The woman wakes alone and counts God's sheep.

11/25

The money-changers of competing thoughts,
Sell talismans of silver and of gold
To represent/broadcast fidelity:
How gracefully you hang on necklace Tree!
Whether I wash my faith-cloth new or old,
Dry in or hang outside for all to see –
Show me the truth, and save me from these "ought's".

11/26

The mime in clownface white who leans on air,
Creates an image stronger than a wall;
On Via Dolorosa, frankincense
Of veneration scents Christ's palm-print there;
And when, like him, we sweat and fear and fall,
When bearing walls collapse/destroy our tents –
The baby-breath of Jesus is our all!

11/27

In silent, snowy fields, grief-seeds are sown.
We have most those we love and must let go,
Whether to freedom/marriage/death – forgive
Me, Lord, that whom you gave I sought to own,
That I might feed on them, not be alone!
Deep in thanksgiving-loss, though old, I know
You will receive this prayer and help me live.

28.

She leaves, but not forsakes. Oft in the night,
Oft at mid-day when all is still around,
Sudden will rise, in dim pathetic light,
Some childish memory of household bliss,
Or sorrow by love's service robed and crowned;
Rich in his love, she yet will sometimes miss
The mother's folding arms, the mother's sealing kiss.

29.

Then first, I think, our eldest-born, although
Loving, devoted, tender, watchful, dear,
The innermost of home-bred love shall know!
Yea, when at last the janitor draws near,
A still, pale joy will through the darkness go,
At thought of lying in those arms again,
Which once were heaven enough for any pain.

30.

By love doth love grow mighty in its love:
Once thou shalt love us, child, as we love thee.
Father of loves, is it not thy decree
That, by our long, far-wandering remove
From thee, our life, our home, our being blest,
We learn at last to love thee true and best,
And rush with all our loves back to thy infinite rest?

11/28

I have forsaken, but I cannot quit
The one who'd have me stay her watchful child,
Whose happiest hours were when I was most small.
I hold my breath to hear her faintest call,
As stone is warmed by worship's chant compiled,
Lot's salty daughter *loves*, who once was wild,
And icon myrrh-tears flood her crust of wit.

11/29

My mother's jawbone sharp upon my back,
She squeaks ecstatically – a stiff embrace.
I set out desperately for Innermost,
Traveling light, scant virtues in my pack.
Past wandering now, a patient, bereft ghost,
I dream no long-lost father's arms or face
Beyond the scythe, just Christ – love, light and host.

11/30

Lord, do revivify this heart grown cold!
Death is not real to me, I am so bent –
I see I cannot love for fear of loss,
Like as child thinking that if I withhold
My deepest love, I can somehow prevent
Love's anguish on inevitable cross.
Why does this Advent feel so much like Lent?

DECEMBER.

1.

I am a little weary of my life —
Not thy life, blessed Father! Or the blood
Too slowly laves the coral shores of thought,
Or I am weary of weariness and strife.
Open my soul-gates to thy living flood;
I ask not larger heart-throbs, vigour-fraught,
I pray thy presence, with strong patience rife.

2.

I will what thou will'st — only keep me sure
That thou art willing; call to me now and then.
So, ceasing to enjoy, I shall endure
With perfect patience — willing beyond my ken
Beyond my love, beyond my thinking scope;
Willing to be because thy will is pure;
Willing thy will beyond all bounds of hope.

3.

This weariness of mine, may it not come
From something that doth need no setting right?
Shall fruit be blamed if it hang wearily
A day before it perfected drop plumb
To the sad earth from off its nursing tree?
Ripeness must always come with loss of might.
The weary evening fall before the resting night.

DECEMBER

12/1

I do not know, Lord, how to love and live
Without the other half of my apple,
And yet I must. Seal now this incomplete,
And guide me by the star of Christ-child; give
Me the key to the heart's winter chapel,
That I may give thee thanks with every beat,
And receive mercy at the justice seat.

12/2

I live in thee without wise certainty –
My prayer and thy call a bramble-rose.
The seeking-revelation blooming grows.
May my breath and thy leading now entwine
Infinite meaning in each tiny sign,
Perfection in each white flake of the snows,
And dawning willingness, deep as can be.

12/3

In heaviness, body and soul, I bear
Several stillborn illusions to the grave
Of winter silence called *Plumb Nelly* by
Combat vet: *plumb* out of state; *nearly* (sigh)
Out the world. Word, Lord, help me to be brave,
And ripen goodness in me; darn this care
With bright red needle of the dragonfly.

4.

Hither if I have come through earth and air,
Through fire and water – I am not of them;
Born in the darkness, what fair-flashing gem
Would to the earth go back and nestle there?
Not of this world, this world my life doth hem;
What if I weary, then, and look to the door,
Because my unknown life is swelling at the core?

5.

All winged things came from the waters first;
Airward still many a one from the water springs
In dens and caves wind-loving things are nursed: –
I lie like unhatched bird, upfolded, dumb,
While all the air is trembling with the hum
Of songs and beating hearts and whirring wings,
That call my slumbering life to wake to happy things.

6.

I lay last night and knew not why I was sad.
"'Tis well with God," I said, "and he is the truth;
Let that content me." – 'Tis not strength, nor youth,
Nor buoyant health, nor a heart merry-mad,
That makes the fact of things wherein men live:
He is the life, and doth my life outgive;
In him there is no gloom, but all is solemn-glad,

7.

I said to myself, "Lo, I lie in a dream
Of separation, where there comes no sign;
My waking life is hid with Christ in God,
Where all is true and potent – fact divine."
I will not heed the thing that doth but seem;
I will be quiet as lark upon the sod;
God's will, the seed, shall rest in me the pod.

12/4

Some sleep in coffins, live in piney pod,
Each night commend their dreams into the vast
Infinitude of Newland where our God
Patiently waits death's harvest, with great love
Shelling us out of humble earthlives past.
Shake off this imagery – "beyond/above";
Comfort me only with thy staff and rod.

12/5

In this cocoon the caterpillar ends,
And we, veil-winged, warmed by the prayer-amens,
Fly straight into the snowstorm, precious, bright.
Christ, righteous, is baptized, the dove descends,
God names and loves his own delightful son;
The flame of sea-cave rainbow candlelight
Within the spirit's wind says we are one.

12/6

As Jesus weeps, sure, God in august gloom
Must marvel at the wildfire wars down here,
And grieve to see his peace be blown apart,
Who sees a child's wet face, a shining tear.
Some sadness in the frozen winter tomb
Is consonant with love/redemptive art,
And thankfulness in prayer of the heart.

12/7

The feather-church of snow enshrouds the cave
Of solitude where I now hibernate.
Here in this myth I have become a bear
Who sleeps through advent warfare: she whose fate
Depends upon blaze orange hat to save
From hunter and from unholy despair.
Lord, send thy baby Jesus – hear our prayer!

8.

And when that will shall blossom – then, my God,
There will be jubilation in a world!
The glad lark, soaring heavenward from the sod,
Up the swift spiral of its own song whirled,
Never such jubilation wild out-poured
As from my soul will break at thy feet, Lord,
Like a great tide from sea-heart shoreward hurled.

9.

For then thou wilt be able, then at last,
To glad me as thou hungerest to do;
Then shall thy life my heart all open find,
A thoroughfare to thy great spirit-wind;
Then shall I rest within thy holy vast,
One with the bliss of the eternal mind;
And all creation rise in me created new.

10.

What makes thy being a bliss shall then make mind
For I shall love as thou, and love in thee;
Then shall I have whatever I desire,
My every faintest wish being all divine;
Power thou wilt give me to work mightily,
Even as my Lord, leading thy low men nigher,
With dance and song to cast their best upon thy fire.

11.

Then shall I live such an essential life
That a mere flower will then to me unfold
More bliss than now grandest orchestral strife –
By love made and obedience humble-bold,
I shall straight through its window God behold.
God, I shall feed on thee, thy creature blest
With very being – work at one with sweetest rest.

12/8

The *fourth* king, Herod, shivers on his throne;
Joseph and Mary head for David's town.
Our cold hopes rise like breath-clouds through ice-doubt.
Light years away, a tiny star, unknown,
Moves slowly through full-moonlight, starting down.
Thanks to God-bearing girl-child's *Yes* devout –
Love will break her chaste seal from inside out!

12/9

O Living God, just now you give me joy
So far beyond imagining, and, too,
The salutary sufferings that make
This *pique-assiette* cracked heart-cup bear the brew
Of water and of blood. O, living boy –
Now Joseph joins Rome's census ("father, Jew") –
New Eve will bring thee forth, that Day may break!

12/10

This gray day I am careful what I wish.
I am too small to drive thy awesome Will;
Would rather, Lord, be guided, hear, and do.
To dare to want is given to the few –
Renunciation seems an advent dish,
A bowl of stone soup will warm us until
The salted fire of Godpeace burns anew.

12/11

Snow melts in rain – so my wish to become
Mystically powerful ebbs, though evergreen.
Thirsty windswept longing like a spring day
In "the bleak midwinter" is my sweet crumb
Of eucharistic bliss today. I lean
My bare branches into the sky – thy way
Wherever it leads in thy wind, I pray.

12.

Give me a world, to part for praise and sunder.
The brooks be bells; the winds, in caverns dumb,
Wake fife and flute and flageolet and voice;
The fire-shook earth itself be the great drum;
And let the air the region's bass out thunder;
The firs be violins; the reeds hautboys;
Rivers, seas, icebergs fill the great score up and under!

13.

But rather dost thou hear the blundered words
Of breathing creatures; the music-lowing herds
Of thy great cattle; thy soft-bleating sheep;
O'erhovered by the trebles of thy birds,
Whose Christ-praised carelessness song-fills the deep;
Still rather a child's talk who apart doth hide him,
And make a tent for God to come and sit beside him.

14.

This is not life; this being is not enough.
But thou art life, and thou hast life for me.
Thou mad'st the worm – to cast the wormy slough,
And fly abroad – a glory flit and flee.
Thou hast me, statue-like, hewn in the rough,
Meaning at last to shape me perfectly.
Lord, thou hast called me forth, I turn and call on thee.

15.

'Tis thine to make, mine to rejoice in thine.
As, hungering for his mother's face and eyes,
The child throws wide the door, back to the wall,
I run to thee, the refuge from poor lies:
Lean dogs behind me whimper, yelp, and whine;
Life lieth ever sick, Death's writhing thrall,
In slavery endless, hopeless, and supine.

12/12

Today, Lord of the lovely earth – great cloud
Flocks sweep slowly east, each precious wind sings
"Hooray! What a day, Master of all things!"
Theotokos rises from a brook, bowed
Inward to her heavy child, who moves! Wings
Of small sparrows in the brush; her brief days
Of childhood close; a Mozart quintet plays.

12/13

As a girl, marveling at the rich earth,
Placing a cobalt glass shard with grave love,
Making a landscape of order, I heard
A small voice say, *"As below, so above"*.
It seemed to me a teaching of great worth:
That my every action and every word
Mattered, in tandem with a grace absurd.

12/14

The snowstorm starts in winds without a sound,
With tiny flakes that seem to fall and rise,
So like the home-made catch-can novice prayers
That fly from us to fall into the skies.
When joined with cloistered warrior-chants world-round,
We blizzard bright Above beyond nay-sayers –
And light the seven lamp-stands by our sighs.

12/15

I longed for father, but found no refuge;
Nor was there brother who would protect me.
My mother lived in Optimism Land;
I saw the dangers she chose not to see,
And killed, for my small sister, dragons huge.
Finally, upon my knees, called Christ the grand –
Now shelter in the hollow of his hand.

16.

The life that hath not willed itself to be,
Must clasp the life that willed, and be at peace;
Or, like a leaf wind-blown, through chaos flee;
A life-husk into which the demons go,
And work their will, and drive it to and fro;
A thing that neither is, nor yet can cease,
Which uncreation can alone release.

17.

But when I turn and grasp the making hand,
And will the making will, with confidence
I ride the crest of the creation-wave,
Helpless no more, no more existence' slave;
In the heart of love's creating fire I stand,
And, love-possessed in heart and soul and sense,
Take up the making share the making Master gave.

18.

That man alone who does the Father's works
Can be the Father's son; yea, only he
Who sonlike can create, can ever *be*;
Who with God wills not, is no son, not free.
O Father, send the demon-doubt that lurks
Behind the hope, out into the abyss;
Who trusts in knowledge all its good shall miss.

19.

Thy beasts are sinless, and do live before thee;
Thy child is sinful, and must run to thee.
Thy angels sin not and in peace adore thee;
But I must will, or never more be free.
I from thy heart came, how can I ignore thee? –
Back to my home I hurry, haste, and flee;
There I shall dwell, love-praising evermore thee.

12/16

The super demons came – I'd swept, new-broom –
Into my "godliness", corroding fears
Made order chaos, damned me with one voice.
Delivery is slow, as Mary knows,
Wondering "How will Joseph find a room?"
Childbirth is messy; water, blood and tears –
Godhead within is ripe through grief: rejoice!

12/17

When kindergarteners cross the busy street
At the signal-light, they cross together,
Each holds a rope-loop, teacher in the lead.
As Mary rides toward Bethlehem, the heat
Of the donkey warms her, the living seed
Of the Holy Spirit is her tether;
Her giving and receiving will soon meet.

12/18

It's *acts* of the apostles, yet, being,
Receiving, comprehending, listening –
These are daughters' works – saying *Yes*, seeing;
The wedding miracle (earth-maid-divine)
Sufficient to change water into wine.
Later, faith turns wine to blood, glistening
Penitential tears become hope benign.

12/19

Thy girl, whether I will or just assent –
I feel thee, Holy Child, within, you lead
By hiccup, gentle pressure, or sharp poke.
I set my cap for some wrong zone or heed
Closed doors, bold/subtle signs; a foolish joke
Strikes to the bone. I am thy green-stick, bent,
Half-broken, turning dowser, bruiséd reed.

20.

My holy self, thy pure ideal, lies
Calm in thy bosom, which it cannot leave;
My self unholy, no ideal, hies
Hither and thither, gathering store to grieve –
Not now, O Father! now it mounts, it flies,
To join the true self in thy heart that waits,
And, one with it, be one with all the heavenly mates.

21.

Trusting thee, Christ, I kneel, and clasp thy knee;
Cast myself down, and kiss thy brother-feet –
One self thou and the Father's thought of thee!
Ideal son, thou hast left the perfect home,
Ideal brother, to seek thy brothers come!
Thou know'st our angels all, God's children sweet,
And of each two wilt make one holy child complete.

22.

To a slow end I draw these daily words,
Nor think such words often to write again –
Rather, as light the power to me affords,
Christ's new and old would to my friends unbind;
Through words he spoke help to his thought behind;
Unveil the heart with which he drew his men;
Set forth his rule o'er devils, animals, corn, and wind.

23.

I do remember how one time I thought,
"God must be lonely – oh, so lonely lone!
I will be very good to him – ah, nought
Can reach the heart of his great loneliness!
My whole heart I will bring him, with a moan
That I may not come nearer; I will lie prone
Before the awful loveliness in loneliness' excess."

12/20

Past Christmas echoes rise up with the sun,
My exploits evidence I can't outrun.
I lick each envelope, apply each stamp,
Hang doilies, string cranberries, cut the stem
Of a dark red rose beside an old lamp
Shining on an address-book – mournful fun –
As Mary enters into Bethlehem.

12/21

Vibrating like the cartoon cat just brained
By an iron frying pan: so many
Emotional reverberations – ten,
Seven, four, two – one bereft child remained
Under the grown-ups' table. If any
Crumb of wisdom falls into my playpen,
I pounce. Have I faith yet? *If not now, when?*

12/22

Time now to thresh the word-seed you have sown
One hundred twenty-seven years ago
In these white pages, in our minds and hearts.
May these responses root through snow and grow
In spirit to bestir new friends unknown.
Water breaks; Virgin's holy labor starts,
Through blood and light toward such a lowly throne.

12/23

Mary is lonely as a budded rose,
Soon she will bear the Holy Spirit child,
Deliver him who's born to free the world.
This is the first of many letting-go's,
Blood of her blood, flesh of her flesh, she knows
Like Eve, the first child-birth; keen pain, then mild
Peace, from confinement blooms, wee fists unfurled.

24.

A God must have a God for company.
And lo! thou hast the Son-God to thy friend.
Thou honour'st his obedience, he thy law.
Into thy secret life-will he doth see;
Thou fold'st him round in live love perfectly –
One two, without beginning, without end;
In love, life, strength, and truth, perfect without a flaw.

25.

Thou hast not made, or taught me, Lord, to care
For times and seasons – but this one glad day
Is the blue sapphire clasping all the lights
That flash in the girdle of the year so fair –
When thou wast born a man, because alway
Thou wast and art a man, through all the flights
Of thought, and time, and thousandfold creation's play.

26.

We all are lonely, Maker – each a soul
Shut in by itself, a sundered atom of thee.
No two yet loved themselves into a whole;
Even when we weep together we are two.
Of two to make one, which yet two shall be,
Is thy creation's problem, deep, and true,
To which thou only hold'st the happy, hurting clue.

27.

No less than thou, O Father, do we need
A God to friend each lonely one of us.
As touch not in the sack two grains of seed,
Touch no two hearts in great worlds populous.
Outside the making God we cannot meet
Him he has made our brother: homeward, thus,
To find our kin we first must turn our wandering feet.

12/24

These tears are ornaments upon the tree;
Slow as snails, watering all dry regret.
A sigh of prayers unspoken joins the wind
That melts the snows and floods the salty sea.
This swaddling-cloth, woven by those who've sinned,
We give, before the Three Kings come to thee –
May it bless/clothe the *Wonder* you beget!

12/25

Deep (in borrowed solitude) as a nail
In the plain, pinewood coffin of vain love,
I am Rachel – such grief cannot be fixed.
I twinkle: on this barren fig tree, a dove
Ornament, made in China, its smile mixed
With sad gratitude, shines. Within, a veil
Of lace lifts: here is the Child, born above!

12/26

"The other half of the apple" – just so
My false true-love described me, and I bit.
The poison lingers; still, with every red,
Green and pink one, with *pommes de terre*, I know:
Slice whole in two, create the perfect fit.
God's heart beats here. Alone in narrow bed,
I turn toward Adam's rib in joy and woe.

12/27

Make my light shine, if you must trim my wick.
Bear with me, God, despite my comic *schtick*.
Sometimes we more than touch, and porous are –
Exchange/seed energies in silence, sighs –
Raise lonely hearts to find (at night's north star,
Along the roads of journeys near and far)
Home, sweet home in a total stranger's eyes.

28.

It must be possible that the soul made
Should absolutely meet the soul that makes;
Then, in that bearing soul, meet every other
There also born, each sister and each brother.
Lord, till I meet thee thus, life is delayed;
I am not I until that morning breaks,
Not I until my consciousness eternal wakes.

29.

Again I shall behold thee, daughter true;
The hour will come when I shall hold thee fast
In God's name, loving thee all through and through.
Somewhere in his grand thought this waits for us.
Then shall I see a smile not like thy last –
For that great thing which came when all was past,
Was not a smile, but God's peace glorious.

30.

Twilight of the transfiguration-joy,
Gleam-faced, pure-eyed, strong-willed, high-hearted boy!
Hardly thy life clear forth of heaven was sent,
Ere it broke out into a smile, and went.
So swift thy growth, so true thy goalward bent,
Thou, child and sage inextricably blent,
Wilt one day teach thy father in some heavenly tent

31.

Go, my beloved children, live your life.
Wounded, faint, bleeding, never yield the strife.
Stunned, fallen-awake, arise, and fight again.
Before you victory stands, with shining train
Of hopes not credible until they *are*.
Beyond morass and mountain swells the star
Of perfect love – the home of longing heart and brain

12/28

We wait for the shoe with the bomb to drop.
Holy innocents, slain in earthquakes, wars –
Are mourned by survivors, the walking dead.
These are our brothers and sisters, the bread
Broken for us; marrow-bones carved as oars
To row our festooned Christmas barge. We stop,
Say Grace, swab decks, and plant the apple cores.

12/29

Cuckolded by the power of God's peace,
I hold my father's death-mask in my heart,
And always full-stop in the street to see
Daughters and fathers in sweet harmony.
When time begins again, we'll do our part
To live through into hope, past love's release,
Into reunion's prayer without cease.

12/30

A wraith amidst the company of those
Conceiving, bearing, bringing forth a child
Whom God gives them to love, then takes right back!
Yet these earth angels can raise hope from wild
Fathomless grief. I am not fit to close
This year among them. Yet, through the sharp crack
In my armor, God blooms one blood-red rose!

12/31

Through new white pages God-with-us shines clear!
Ah, bless us, Old Soul, as you touch us here,
Trembling upon the cusp of this New Year.
We do aspire to all you have attained;
With gratitude which cannot be contained,
Thanks for your guidance each and every day.
May we be singing shells upon thy Way!

Christ, who well knowest why my lips are sealed –
Knowest my wrath, and my proud sense of wrong :
One word of thine a comfort sad doth yield,
Makes me with pardoning endurance strong,
And hope of cleansing sorrow on its way :
That "nought is covered but shall be revealed,
And nothing hid but shall be known one day."

What must it be in perfect trust to keep
Still in the world, in Christ confiding all;
To give up everything, to hope, to fail,
To sow waiting itself, to dare look deep
Within the husk, Old Soul, both rise and fall
At the well of the one immortal grail,
Hearing with golden ears the sacred call?

March 8.

Be with me, Lord. Keep me beyond all prayers:
For more than all my prayers my need of thee,
And thou beyond all need, all unknown cares;
What the heart's dear imagination dares,
Thou dost transcend in measureless majesty
All prayers in one – my God, be unto me
Thy own eternal self, absolutely.

January 25 - 26

Not in my fancy now I search to find thee;
Not in its loftiest forms would shape or bind thee;
I cry to one whom I can never know,
Filling me with an infinite overflow;
Not to a shape that dwells within my heart,
Clothed in perfections love and truth assigned thee,
But to the God thou knowest that thou art.

Not, Lord, because I have done well or ill;
Not that my mind looks up to thee clear-eyed;
Not that it struggles in fast cerements tied;
Not that I need thee daily sorer still;
Not that I, wretched, wander from thy will;
Not now for any cause to thee I cry,
But this, that thou art thou, and here am I.

March 8.

Be with me, Lord. Keep me beyond all prayer:
For more than all my prayer my need of thee,
And thou beyond all need, all unknown cares;
What the heart's dear imagination dares,
Thou dost transcend in measureless majesty.
All prayer in one — my God, be unto me
Thy own eternal self, absolutely.

January 15-26

Not in my fancy now I search to find thee;
Not in its loftiest forms would shape or bind thee;
I cry to one whom I can never know,
Filling me with an infinite overflow;
Not to a shape that dwells within my heart,
Clothed in perfection's love and truth assured thee
But to the God thou knowest that thou art.
Not, Lord, because I have done well or ill;
Not that my mind looks up to thee clear-eyed
Not that it struggles in thick cerements tied
Not that I need thee daily sorer still;
Not that I wretched, wander from thy will
Not now for any cause to thee I cry,
But this, that thou art thou, and here am I.

These MacDonald prayer/poems, in the handwriting of Paul Rogness, were found in his pocket after his death in an auto accident. They inspired his father, Alvin, to bring *Diary* back into print in the Augsburg Publishing edition of 1975, and are included here by kind permission of his brother, Michael Rogness.

ENDNOTES

Epigraphs:

William Butler Yeats – introduction to *Crossways* (1889), an adaptation of William Blake's "And all Nations were threshed out & the stars threshd from their husks" from *The Four Zoas: Vala - Night the Ninth Being The Last Judgment.*

Dylan Thomas – from *A Refusal to Mourn the Death, by Fire, of a Child in London.*

JANUARY

1/1   (lines 3 & 4)   "Throughout all ages, world without end." – Eph. iii.

1/2   *shiva*: A seven-day period of formal mourning observed after the funeral of a close relative. [from the Hebrew šibʻâ, seven.]

1/4   *Tao* – In Confucianism, the right manner of human activity and virtuous conduct seen as stemming from universal criteria and ideals governing right and wrong.

1/8   The Jesus Prayer: in the Eastern Orthodox tradition: a short prayer the words of which are: "Lord Jesus Christ, Son of God, have mercy on me, a sinner." see *Franny & Zoey* by J.D. Salinger, *The Way of the Pilgrim* and *The Philokalia.*

1/9   (line 1) title song of the 1949 musical *Lost in the Stars*, book and lyrics by Maxwell Anderson, music by Kurt Weill.
        (line 7) Psalm 121:4 – see also "He watching over Israel, slumbers not nor sleeps." – from *Elijah* by Felix Mendelssohn.

1/14   (line 4) Psalm 51:10; also see John Michael and Terry Talbot's song "Create in me a clean heart, O Lord" from *The Painter.*

1/21   (lines 1,2 & 4) Romans 11:15, 16, 23 & 24

1/23   mobius - a continuous one-sided surface that can be formed from a rectangular strip by rotating one end 180° and attaching it to the other end.

1/25   (line 6) from "Even Me" by Mrs. Elizabeth Codner, leaflet (1896), hymn, and gospel standard; and Esau's tears, Genesis 27:38

FEBRUARY

2/3   (lines 2-3) *Meditations on the Tarot: A Guide to Christian Hermeticism.* p.548
        (line 7) "Holy Fire": Heavenly fire ignites all the lamps in the Church of the Holy Sepulchre in Jerusalem on Holy Saturday, the day preceding Orthodox Easter. This is the longest annual miracle in the Christian world, consecutively documented since 1106.

2/4   (line 7) "crucified, wed, sealed" Bride of the Crucified: "The bridal union of the soul with God is the end for which she was created: bought by the Cross, consummated on the cross, and for all eternity sealed with the cross." *The Science of the Cross* by Edith Stein/St. Benedicta of the Cross.

2/14   see also 2/27 and 3/2

2/19   "It is easier for a camel to go through the eye of a needle than for a rich man to enter the kingdom of God." Matthew 19:24

2/20   *Meditations on the Tarot: A Guide to Christian Hermeticism.* p.456

2/27   "Under the Mercy" – phrase on Charles Williams' tombstone; Fred M. Rogers d. 2/27/03.

2/28   Psalm 55:6

2/29   (line 1) *pique-assiette*: broken shards of crockery reconfigured into a mosaic creation of something new.

MARCH

3/3   "all the world's a stage" Shakespeare, *As You Like It.*

3/4   The story of *Cupid and Psyche* was transformed in C.S. Lewis' *Till We Have Faces.*

3/6   (lines 1-4) "If you are willing to bear with serenity the trial of being displeasing to yourself, then you will be for Jesus a pleasant place of shelter."
– St. Thérèse of Lisieux (The Little Flower)

3/14   *Agape*: Love as revealed in Jesus, seen as spiritual and selfless.

3/19   (line 1) "Nebuchadnezzar", a print by William Blake (1757 - 1827)

3/21   (line 2) *The Habit of Being* – letters of Flannery O'Connor.

3/25   On March 20th, 2003, the United States invaded Iraq and has been occupying it.

3/27   (line 7) thy miracles seven: ... at the wedding of Cana, healing of the nobleman's son, healing of the paralyzed man at the pool of Bethesda, the feeding of the five thousand, the walking on the water, the healing of the man born blind, & the raising of Lazarus at Bethany, described in the Gospel according to John. *Meditations on the Tarot, A Journey into Christian Hermeticism.* p 150

3/28   (line 5) The Just: ancient legend that the world is saved from folly/wickedness by the presence in each generation of a small number of righteous beings who, through their virtue, conduct, and deeds, ensure the safety and survival of the people. They operate inconspicuously: scarcely recognized by others or even themselves. Proverbs X praises the Just as the everlasting foundation of the world.

3/29   (line 1) Matthew 26:39. Mark 14:36, Luke22:42

3/31   (lines 5 & 6) re. "Eloi, Eloi, lama sabachthani?" "My God, my God, why hast thou forsaken me?" Psalm 22:1, Matthew 27:46

APRIL

4/5   (line 3) see endnote, 1/23
        (lines 6 & 7) Luke 23:43

4/9   (line 3) Psalm 23:5
        (line 7) In Greek myth, Europa is carried away by Zeus (disguised as a white bull) across the sea to a distant land.

4/10　　(line 1)　John 9:1-11
　　　　　(line 2)　the idea taught in ultra-Orthodox yeshiva (school), that Jewish women serve God by having sons and being 'footstools' to their husbands in heaven after death (also Matthew 5:34.35).
　　　　　(line 3)　Luke 8:41-48
　　　　　(line 4)　Genesis 24:1-9, 47:29

4/11　　(line 2)　Gulliver is tied down by Lilliputians in *Gulliver's Travels* by Jonathan Swift.

4/14　　Maundy Thursday: (the washing of the feet, John 13).

4/15　　(line 1)　popular radio/television show in the 1950s; Matthew 23:9

4/17 -　(line 1)　Bruised Moses: Exodus 4:10; Isaiah 42:3; Psalm 51:17
　　　　　sea of reeds: in the Septuagint translation of the book of Exodus, the Hebrew word meaning Reed Sea, is translated as Erythra Thalassa (Red Sea).
　　　　　(line 2)　Consecrated firstborns: Luke 2:23
　　　　　　　　　　unleavened: as matzo, Exodus 12:12,15,29,39
　　　　　(line 4)　*Pesach*: Jewish Passover, Elijah's seder cup, Last Supper
　　　　　(line 5)　*Pascha*: Christian Easter, Feast of the Resurrection
　　　　　(line 6)　Maundy Thursday: the washing of the feet, John 13
　　　　　　　　　　narded feet: the anointing, Luke 7:36-50
　　　　　(line 7)　the Mercy seat: once a year, on Yom Kippur, the Jewish high priest entered into the Holy of Holies to sprinkle the blood of the bull on the mercy seat for the atonement of the people. Christians (Hebrews 9, 10) assert that Christ becomes both high priest and sacrifice.

4/18　　(line 1) from Howard Nemerov's book of poetry *The Next Room Of The Dream.*

4/19　　(line 2)　from Dar Williams' song "The Mercy of the Fallen."

4/25　　(line 1)　Matt 13:24-30; 36-43
　　　　　(line 2 & 3)　Luke 10:38-42

4/30　　(line 6)　birth, baptism, death.

MAY

5/1　　(line 3)　ceaseless prayer: Thessalonians 5:17

5/8   "Death deepens the wonder." – Tillie Olsen, *Tell Me A Riddle*;
"The job of the artist is always to deepen the mystery." – Francis Bacon

5/13   line 4) monastic custom called "custody of the eyes". To facilitate
unceasing prayer, monastics keep their gaze lowered, minimizing
unnecessary visual temptations/distractions that might fragment or divert
their attention.

5/19   (line 5) John 4:4-42
         (line 7) John 19:26-27

5/21   (line 7) "His Eye Is On The Sparrow" by Civilla D. Martin & Charles
Gabriel, a hymn made famous by Ethel Waters. Matthew 10:29 & 6:26

5/23   (line 7) "thy rod and thy staff they comfort me" Psalm 23:4

5/26   (line 1) "when the old lambs are shorn, the little ones tremble." old
Yiddish proverb.

5/28   GMD: (line 4) "pelf" - n. Wealth or riches, especially when
dishonestly acquired.

5/30   (line 4) Exodus 14:21,22
         (line 7) "Receive the Body of Christ. Taste the Fountain of
Immortality." Eastern Orthodox Communion of the People, Divine Liturgy
of Saint John Chrysostom.

JUNE

6/3   (line 3) "to pull someone's coat" – urban slang – to inform or teach,
give knowledgeable advice.
         (line 6) Luke 10:42.
         (line 7) Matthew 13:24-30,36-43

6/11   (line 7) *Winnie the Pooh and Eeyore's House* by A.A. Milne

6/12   (line 1) "The Second Coming" by William Butler Yeats
         (line 4) "Treason doth never prosper: what's the reason?
                   Why, if it prosper, none dare call it treason."
                   from *Epigrams*, by Sir John Harrington. (1561–1612)

6/14   (line 4) "There is a balm in Gilead to make the wounded whole; There is a balm in Gilead to heal the sin sick soul."; classic Spiritual.

6/15   (line 7) Father's Day celebrated in the United States in June

6/16   (line 1) a fairy tale adapted by the Brothers Grimm, in which Hansel with white pebbles, and later breadcrumbs, seeks to mark his way home.
        (line 4) Psalm 23:4

6/17   (line 7) "Jesus answered and said unto her, If thou knowest the gift of God, and who it is that saith to thee, Give me to drink; thou wouldest have asked of him, and he would have given thee living water." John 4:10

6/21   (line 1) *Le Pendu*: The Hanged Man, 12th card of the Major Arcana, suspended up-side-down: " ..the 'solid ground' under his feet is found above, whilst the ground below is only the concern and perception of his head". *Meditations on the Tarot: A Guide to Christian Hermeticism.*

6/22   (line 3) "to see eternity in a grain of sand." - William Blake

6/26   (line 5) *Je t'aime*: French, I love you.

6/30   (line 1) Nazi concentration camps/crematoriums
        (lines 2-7) Hans Christian Andersen: *The Little Mermaid* (1837), *The Wild Swans* (1838), *The Red Shoes* (1845).

JULY

7/1   (line 5) "Patriot Act:" warrantless spying by the government instituted in response to 9/11.

7/3   (line 1) 1 Corinthians 13:12
        (line 2) splinters of the devil's mirror in Hans Christian Andersen's *The Snow Queen* - get into the eye, shrinking the good and beautiful to nothing; magnifying the worthless and ugly, freezing the heart.

7/4   (line 2) lobelia: a dark blue flower.

7/7   (line 1) *A Severe Mercy* by Sheldon Vanauken

7/8   (line 4) In MacDonald's original 1880 edition, he uses the Scottish word "teal" (meaning "tricks, cajoles") but later editions use the word "steal."

7/9   (line 1) "To Everything There Is a Season", song by Pete Seeger from Ecclesiastes 3:1-8; also "Simple Gifts", traditional Shaker song.
         (line 6) Psyche is given three impossible tasks by Venus in the myth.

7/13   (line 5) troglodyte: member of a prehistoric cave-dwelling race of people; person considered to be reclusive, reactionary, out of date, or brutish.
         (line 7) Ezekiel 1:10; Revelations 4:7 – the Evangelists, the cross

7/15   (line 4) "God speed the plough" – a wish for success, originally a phrase in a 15th-century song sung by ploughmen on Plough Monday, the first Monday after Twelfth Day, at the end of the Christmas holidays, when farm laborers returned to the plough.

7/21   "Mother, may I go out to swim? Yes, my darling daughter.
           Hang your cloths on a hickory limb, but don't go near the water."

7/29   (line 6) *yeshiva*: an institution for Torah study and the study of Talmud primarily within Orthodox Judaism.
         Matthew 13:24-30,36-43

7/30   (line 1) the secret place: Psalm 91:1

AUGUST

8/2   (line 1) A sign over the entrance to Auschwitz (the complex including concentration extermination and forced-labor camps) read *ARBEIT MACHT FREI*, meaning "work makes one free." In actuality, the opposite was true. Labor became another form of genocide that the Nazis called "extermination through work."

8/3   In Macdonald's poem, "Sychar" refers to Jacob's well. (Genesis 13:18-19) and in John 4:5-26, Jesus asks the Samarian woman for water.

8/7   (line 1) *Prince Igor* - by Alexander Porfiryevich Borodin (1833-1887)
         (line 3) super - a supernumerary - one who has a small acting, non-singing, part in an opera.

8/9   (line 1) John 19:29

8/10   (line 6) Luke 22:18 "For I say unto you, I will not drink of the fruit of the vine until the kingdom of God shall come." See also Scott Hahn's article "The Hunt for the Forth Cup," *This Rock* , Vol. 2 #4, September 1991

8/11   (line 4) - *A Refusal to Mourn the Death, by Fire, of a Child in London*, by Dylan Thomas.

8/14   In Greek mythology, Icarus flew too close to the sun, his artificial wax wings melted, and he fell to his death.

8/16   Luke 10:38-42

8/22   (line 1) Luke 22:19 & John 24:30,31
        (line 2) Mark 2:27

8/29   (line 1) ovens = crematoriums of Nazi Extermination Camps: Chelmno, Auschwitz-Birkenau, Belzek, Sobibor, Treblinka, Majdanek, Stutthof

SEPTEMBER

9/5   (line 4) *The Habit of Being: Letters of Flannery O'Connor*

9/7   (line 7) *The Long Loneliness* by Dorothy Day / "Never Alone" a traditional Gospel song.

9/13   (line 1) from "Mother Goose's Melodies" (1833).

9/18   (lines 3 & 4) from an image by Antoine de Saint-Exupery

9/19   (line 2) Romans 11:11-24

9/24   (line 3) from *Sculpting in Time: Tarkovsky The Great Russian Filmaker Discusses His Art* by Andrei Tarkovsky.

9/29   (line 3) "A gentle answer turns away wrath, but a harsh word stirs up anger." Proverbs 15:1
        (line 7) "My sheep know my voice, and I know them, and they follow me" (John 10:27)

9/30   (line 3) "plus three" – The other three deadly sins are sloth, wrath, and pride.

OCTOBER

10/9   (line 4) Beulah Land: a celestial garden bordering on the River of Death in *Pilgrim's Progress from This World to That Which Is To Come* (1678) by John Bunyon

10/11   (line 7) in Matthew 27:7; land unfit to grow crops, therefore only used by potters to dig clay. The place where unclaimed bodies are buried.

10/19   (line 7) "The Holy Fire:" (see endnote on 2/3)

10/21   (line 2) the tolls: Eastern Orthodox belief that after death a soul attempting to ascend into heaven will receive preliminary judgement, trials and temptations at the place called the toll houses.

NOVEMBER

11/8   "Simple Gifts: an 1848 traditional Shaker dancing song by Elder Joseph Brackett (1797-1882)
　　　　　　　'Tis the gift to be simple, 'tis the gift to be free,
　　　　　　　'Tis the gift to come down where we ought to be,
　　　　　　　And when we find ourselves in the place just right,
　　　　　　　'Twill be in the valley of love and delight.
　　　　　　　When true simplicity is gain'd,
　　　　　　　To bow and to bend we shan't be asham'd,
　　　　　　　To turn, turn will be our delight,
　　　　　　　Till by turning, turning we come round right.

11/16   "one in essence and undivided" ref. Byzantine Divine Liturgy of St John Chrysostom.

11/19   (line 7) folksong *I Know Where I'm Going*

11/21   Christ's seven "I am" revelations: The True Vine, The Way the Truth and the Life, The Door, The Bread of Life, The Good Shepherd, The Light of the World, The Resurrection and the Life. *Meditations on the Tarot: A Guide to Christian Hermeticism.* p.150

(line 6) *come round right* "Gift to be Simple" Shaker song.
(line 7) ref. "Everything That Rises Must Converge" : Teilhard de Chardin. Also a short story of the same name by Flannery O'Connor

DECEMBER

12/3   Plumb Nelly: "plum out of town and nelly out of this world" to suggest that the location is so remote it has almost left the map entirely.

12/10   (line 6) In the folktale *Stone Soup*, the villagers at first refuse to contribute food to a soup and finally there is enough to feed the entire village.
(line 7) *Salted by Fire* by George MacDonald

12/12   *Theotokos*: Godbearer

12/21   (line 7)   "If I am not for myself, who will be?
                     If I am only for myself, what am I?
                     And if not now, when?"
                                             Hillel

Gratitudes

My mother, my younger sister and I, secular Jews, belonged to no community. Our liturgies were lullabyes, folksongs and Spirituals. Sacred works were announced by the fatherly voices of radio announcers, a continuous forcefield of classical music. My own father had quit the family, leaving a television in his place. I sought solace in music and art. My nursery rhymes were by William Blake and A.A. Milne. *Cupid and Psyche* was my favorite myth, and I especially loved Hans Christian Andersen, whose stories I devoured. Icons and holy relics were preserved in The Museum of Modern Art; paintings were prayers. My religious formation was the discipline of the dance class, my catechism an endless stream of library books, my communion the drama workshop, my meditation the potter's wheel, my congregation the audience, and my denomination the musical theater. My confessional was the white page of the diary. I wanted, as a child, to "become myself in spite of myself."

The consolations of tv's *Kukla, Fran and Ollie*, and the benedictions of Menotti's *Amahl and The Night Visitor* were profound. After seeing the film version of *The Red Shoes*, I held on tightly to a girder of the Third Avenue El, sobbing inconsolably. The subway labyrinths and sidewalks of New York City offered their lessons of social inequity and danger.

Like Celia, a character in T.S. Eliot's play *The Cocktail Party*, it was devastating rejection/salutary disillusionment – utter failure in love that brought me finally to my knees. As the Father-God was both remote and impossible to relate to, given my lack, I began to pour my heart out to an imagined, loving, approachable, radical, Jewish older Brother in whom I did not yet believe, who might possibly hear me, and understand that I could in no way forgive myself, nor achieve any respite from the torment of my sins.

My debt to those souls, sung and unsung, who illumined my way out of the underworld is beyond measure:

Daisy K. Aberlin, Tillie Olsen, Grace Paley, Shirley Jackson, Flannery O'Connor, Simone Weil, Edith Stein, Dorothy Day, Mabel Mercer; Philip Roth, Isaac Babel, Bernard Malamud, Howard Nemerov, J.D. Salinger, F. M. Rogers, C.S.Lewis, Charles Williams, Graham Greene, Lenny Bruce, Thomas Merton, Kevin Smith, Terry Gilliam, Andrei Tarkovsky, William Sloane Coffin, who baptized me to a hymn Hitler had appropriated for a marching song, Joan Soles of St. Michael's Byzantine Catholic Church and the chapel of C-95, Riker's Island, the Abbess and sisters, Convent of Mary Magdalene, Jerusalem – all who hung the moon until I could be led to *The Light Princess* – most particularly to the members of the online Wingfold community, who sustained and encouraged my efforts, offering loving prayers; and to Robert Trexler who believed in these poems and published them! –

with thanks for the precious being of George MacDonald,
and for the breath of this communion beyond time,
this book is humbly offered
under the mercy
of the one
God.

+

✡

Betty K. Aberlin
December 2007

"*What we do is so little we may seem to be constantly failing.*
But so did He fail. He met with apparent failure on the Cross.
But unless the seed fall into the earth and die, there is no harvest.
And why must we see results? Our work is to sow.
Another generation will be reaping the harvest."

Dorothy Day

CPSIA information can be obtained at www.ICGtesting.com
Printed in the USA
BVOW011836090712

294746BV00007B/62/A

9 780972 322140